Peggy Amend

THE TRIAL

THE TRIAL

A NOVEL BY LINDSEY PHILLIP DEW

DESERET BOOK COMPANY
SALT LAKE CITY, UTAH

This is a work of fiction. Characters described in this book are the products of the author's imagination or are represented fictitiously.

Visit us at deseretbook.com

First printing in paperbound edition, August 1988

Library of Congress Cataloging-in-Publication Data

Dew, Lindsey Phillip.
  The trial.
  I. Title.
  ISBN 0-87747-874-0 (hardbound ed.)
  ISBN-10 0-87579-157-3 (paperbound ed.)
  ISBN-13 978-0-87579-157-9 (paperbound ed.)
  PS3554.E9287T7 1984
  813'.54   84-12711

Printed in the United States of America
Publisher's Printing, Salt Lake City, UT

10   9   8   7   6   5   4

Dedicated to the memory of my
grandfather John Lindsey, Jr.

When a lawyer is appointed by a court ... to undertake representation of a person unable to obtain counsel, ... he should not seek to be excused from undertaking the representation except for compelling reasons. Compelling reasons do not include such factors as the repugnance of the subject matter of the proceeding, the identity or position of a person involved in the case, [or] the belief of the lawyer that the defendant in a criminal proceeding is guilty.

Utah Code of Professional Responsibility, EC 2-29

Chapter One

The dirt trails that once connected Salt Lake City with the remote Mormon settlements of the West are now concrete and asphalt highways. One of those highways moves south from Salt Lake City and continues through Bluffdale, home of the state prison. It then cuts through Orem, famous for Donny and Marie, and goes through Provo, home of Brigham Young University. The road continues through Springville, famous for its art museum (sometimes it doesn't take much to be famous in Utah). The highway moves through Thistle, famous for its well-watered lawns, and enters Sanpete County, famous for its turkeys.

The road then cuts through Fairview, famous home of the National Shrine to Love and Devotion. It passes through Mount Pleasant, famous for its speed traps. The road continues through Ephraim, Sanpete County's largest town and home of Snow College. The road goes on a few more miles and becomes Main Street in Ammon, which isn't famous for anything.

As you enter the Ammon city limits, the first building you see is Carter's Hardware. Its aging proprietor is one of that vanishing breed of shopkeepers who know how to use everything they sell. By the hardware store is Betty's Home Cooking, a small restaurant as well as the local Trailways bus stop. If you're hungry for good food, don't stop there. If you're not particular about what enters your stomach and if you like to flirt with cute waitresses, it's worth investigating. Next to the restaurant is a small office, with big red lettering on the front window that says "LAW OFFICE." On the door in smaller black letters is written "John J. Lindsey III, Attorney-at-law." From eight to five on weekdays, you'll find me there.

The road continues past four dozen or so small business-es: shops, gas stations, motels, a real estate office, a bank, a small supermarket, a rest home, and a hamburger stand. Roads branch off from Main Street, and these smaller roads are lined with homes. There are two churches in town, but they don't compete for business: both are Mormon.

Ammon is a small town, but it isn't grubby. It is neat, clean, and disciplined, like its inhabitants. Tall shade trees line the wide streets, which are laid out at right angles to each other in traditional "City of Zion" style. Places of business are confined to Main Street, and a small, well-kept park sits in the exact center of town.

I've lived here for a little over a decade, and the town hasn't changed much physically since the day I brought my family from Salt Lake and set up my practice here. But though the town doesn't look much different, after the events of the past year it *feels* different. Or perhaps I'm just the one who changed.

It's difficult to say when the change began, for ideas and perceptions sometimes change slowly, almost unnoticeably, just as the cold days of winter may imperceptibly change to spring. Days and events flow into each other, and often it is only in retrospect that a certain day or a particular event becomes significant.

The earth rests now under a blanket of snow, as it did that evening a year ago. I remember that the sun had already fallen behind the mountains as I helped Mrs. Henderson get into her car. As she drove off, I locked the office door behind me. My breath curled up in wisps of steam, and I exhaled forcefully to see how far the steam would go before disappearing. The air was refreshing rather than chilling, so I carried my overcoat instead of putting it on. It was getting dark enough for the cars passing by to turn on their headlights. One of them slowed down and pulled over next to the curb. The driver rolled down the window and said, "Hi, Bishop. Need a ride home?" It was Bob Collingham, my banker and jogging partner.

"No thanks, Bob. The air feels good, so I think I'll walk."

"Yeah, I wonder why it always seems to warm up before the snow hits? They're saying eight more inches by morning. You going jogging with me tomorrow?"

I grinned. "Not if it snows. I jog for my health, not because I'm crazy."

He bade me farewell and drove off.

I walked two blocks down Main Street, then turned up a side street. My home sits three blocks east of Main Street. It's a large, modern, two-story house with a full basement, covered on the outside with yellow aluminum siding and trimmed in white. Bright light spilled from the front window, silhouetting the nativity scene. A snowman, one arm missing as a result of a recent snowball fight, guarded the front yard.

"I'm home," I sang out as I entered the house. My twelve-year-old daughter, Cindy, glanced up from the book she was reading and gave me a look that plainly suggested, "Big deal." Paul, my ninth grader, looked up from his homework and absently said, "Hi, Dad." Since my loving wife, Carol, had not rushed into my arms the moment I stepped into the house, I knew she must be engaged in a matter of crucial importance. I found her in the nursery, changing my youngest son's diapers. From behind I put my arms around her and gave her a kiss.

Carol was a tall, slender woman with light brown hair that used to be long before I married her but had become progressively shorter through the years. Eight childbirths and twenty years of putting up with me had taken its toll on her, but she was still a good-looking woman.

Carol had a well-deserved reputation for intellectual brilliance (though her reputation for intelligence suffered somewhat when people saw whom she married). Carol's mind had a depth and a breadth that mine lacked. I'm sure that she had had me figured out for years, but she was often beyond my comprehension. Her tastes were as far above me as her thoughts. She appreciated good art and could tell the difference between a Picasso and a third grader's scribblings. She occasionally dragged me off to Salt Lake to see Ballet West or the Utah Symphony, and she pretended to actually enjoy herself. (She *must* have been pretending.) I wouldn't mind the concerts so much except that they'd sometimes play so loud that I'd wake up.

Carol had no appreciation for the important things in life. Though she thought BYU was the only place to attend school, she disagreed with my contention that the temple recommend interview should include the question, "Do you support the BYU football team?" In fact, she would rather read a book than go to the games, a sin of omission for which she would someday surely be held accountable.

I was the hot dog in her filet-mignon life. Occasionally I wondered if the only thing we had in common was that indefinable, incomparable, completely irrational essence called love.

"How did things go today?" Carol asked.

"Pretty good," I replied. "But it looks like Cindy is still disfellowshipping me."

Cindy had scouted the various hiding places in the house. She was upset at what she considered to be the paucity of Christmas gifts for her. She wasn't talking to me. I didn't mind.

"What did the doctor say about Johnny?" I inquired.

"He says that his bone structure is normal and that everything looks fine, so there is no organic reason why he isn't walking. He says that with so many big brothers and sisters who like to carry him around, not to mention two indulgent parents, Johnny has no need to walk on his own. He says that until we make him walk, we shouldn't expect much improvement for a while. Now if you'll hold the little goldbricker, I'll get supper on the table," Carol said, handing me the freshly diapered child.

"OK, kid," I said, putting him on the floor. "No more Mr. Nice Guy. Now walk!"

He raised his arms imploringly and wailed. When Carol was out of earshot, I picked him up again.

When dinner was over, I went Christmas caroling with the Mutual kids. After returning home, I sat on the couch and read *Pinocchio* to my two youngest children. I explained to Susie and Johnny that even though Pinocchio's nose grew everytime he told a lie, in real life it was rare for transgression to be followed immediately by divine retribution. My sermon was interrupted by the squeal of tires outside and then the slamming of a car door. My second son came in through the front door.

"Mark, why didn't you come home with me tonight after the caroling?" I asked.

"I went cruising Main Street for a little while with Chris Brinkman and the guys," he replied.

Kids like Chris Brinkman are the bright hope of the future for criminal defense attorneys. On three occasions, I had accompanied Chris to juvenile court. A few years previously, he had broken into Manti High and smashed two thousand dollars worth of audiovisual equipment. A year later, he was charged with killing the pets of some neighbors. Just six months ago, he had been arrested for throwing eggs from his car at other cars. But Chris had recently turned eighteen. The next time, he wouldn't be going to juvenile court.

However, whenever Chris was at our house or around me or my wife, he was always well behaved. He often accompanied my family to various ward activities and outings. Mark told me that Chris once said that he wished he were in our family. I was secretly glad that he wasn't. Because of his well-deserved reputation, I found it hard to trust him and was always concerned that he might lead my son astray.

"Mark, do you have that book report done yet?" I asked.

"Not yet."

"Then you'd better get on it."

"Dad," Mark inquired, "can a cop pull a car over for nothing?"

"Some officer pulled you over?"

"Yeah, a big fat blimp I hadn't seen before pulled us over and drilled us."

I put down the book and said irritably, "I don't like your

language. If you had come home with me when you should have, you wouldn't have had any trouble."

Mark turned around and went downstairs.

"John, he asked you a question."

I looked over at my wife.

"If you light into him everytime he asks you a question, he's going to stop asking."

I felt a twinge of guilt. Mark was always irritating me. He wasn't a bad kid and had never been in any trouble, but I guess I compared him to his older brother and sister. Mark didn't appear to have any ambition and didn't seem to do anything but bum around with his friends, play Atari in his bedroom, and listen to his stereo. Matthew and Brenda, my oldest children, had graduated high in their classes and had been involved heavily in extracurricular activities. Mark would be lucky to graduate in the middle of his class and never got involved in school activities.

Mark and I used to get along really well. Until a few years ago, I had accepted his mediocre grades, believing that he simply wasn't as bright as his brothers and sisters. Then in his sophomore year, he made a terrible mistake. On the aptitude test given to all sophomores, he not only did better than anyone in his class, he did better than anyone at Manti High had ever done. He blew his cover. As far as I was concerned, he was squandering his talents. Mark rarely studied, did his chores at home listlessly, and, though he never shirked his Church responsibilities, he never volunteered for anything extra, either.

The previous summer it had appeared for a while that Mark was changing his ways. Ever since Matthew turned fifteen, he had worked in the summer with my brother Ryan, a general contractor in Salt Lake. After his junior year, Mark had finally been prevailed upon to go also. The initial reports were encouraging. Ryan told me that as good a worker as Matthew was, Mark was even better and learned faster. I had hoped that Mark had finally found himself. But halfway through the summer, Mark suddenly quit, leaving the work crew a man short. It turned out that Mark was only after enough money to buy himself an Atari video game set, a color TV, and game cartridges. As soon as he had the money, he quit and spent the rest of the summer in his room blasting alien life forms. Ryan was really disturbed that Mark would leave him short-handed. Mark didn't appear to care that he had upset his uncle and disappointed his dad. It seemed to be Mark's philosophy to do just as little as he had to do to get by.

But Carol had spoken the truth; it was up to me to keep the lines of communication open. Carol had been valedictorian of the College of Child Development and Family Relations at BYU, and she knew how to raise kids. I put the baby down and went downstairs to Mark's room.

When I opened his door, the low throb of music became a raucous clamor. I was glad Matthew had finished the room off with acoustic ceiling tile, helping to keep peace in the family.

Because Matthew had finished the room and Mark had refused to help, Matthew had justly considered the room to be his. Mark was merely a tenant at sufferance while Matthew was at BYU and in Salt Lake. Responding to Matt's threats, Mark hadn't changed the room much. Books by Steinbeck, Shakespeare, Twain, Buck, Bellow, Hemingway, and Solzhenitsyn jostled each other for space on the crowded shelves. There were a number of books about World War II, several Church books, and even some anti-Mormon literature. On the walls hung a BYU pennant, a Manti High pennant, a few athletic ribbons (for participation, not for accomplishment), and a tiny snapshot of a former girlfriend sitting behind a typewriter. Mark's only additions to the room were a stereo, an Atari set with a TV, and a large poster of Farrah Fawcett.

Mark was lying on his bed, staring at the ceiling.

"Can I turn this down?" I yelled, trying to be heard over the music. Mark nodded his head. I turned the volume down all the way. "I'm sorry I lit into you like that," I apologized.

Mark gave me a friendly smile. He never seemed to hold a grudge.

"What was the problem you were trying to tell me about?" Mark sat up on the edge of his bed.

"Well, Dad, we were just driving up and down Main Street, like we usually do, not speeding or holding up traffic or anything, and this cop pulled us over."

"Did he say why?" I inquired.

Mark shook his head. "No, he just acted like a real big shot. He kept calling us a 'bunch of punks' and stuff like that. And we weren't talking back to him or anything. Then he says, 'I think I'll just run the whole bunch of you into jail and let you spend the night.' So when he said that, Arnie started crying, and Chris says, 'You can't do that!' And the cop says, 'You just watch me!'"

"Who was there?" I asked.

"Just me and Chris and Arnie and Dave."

"Who was driving?"

"Chris was. Well, when the cop saw that Arnie was crying, he got a little nicer and said he'd let us go this time but that he'd keep an eye on us. He said that we'd better watch our step and get haircuts. He didn't want to see us driving around after dark anymore. Can he do that?"

"Who was the officer?"

"Some guy I hadn't seen before. His name tag said 'Frost.'"

"What's his first name? Any idea?"

"I dunno—Jack maybe." Mark grinned.

"Was he city police or county sheriff?"

"Ammon city police."

"Are you sure you weren't doing anything—no speeding, or yelling at people on the street, or throwing things again, or anything like that?"

"Honest, Dad, we weren't. After Chris got arrested for throwing eggs at cars, he's kind of calmed down, and the rest of us have never done anything like that."

"I'll talk to Chief Reitzen next time I see him. If some new officer on his force is harassing kids, I think he'll want to know."

"But can he do like he says—throw us in jail for nothing?"

I shook my head. "An officer isn't even supposed to pull you over unless he has a reason to believe that you've violated the law. He's probably some new guy who's let power go to his head. Chief Reitzen will take care of him. But listen, if he pulls you guys over again, don't sass him or tell him he can't do anything to you. Just act sorry and try to get away from him, then come to tell me. Chief Reitzen will give any new guy a chance or two, but if he gets a lot of complaints, he won't hesitate to fire an officer. So let me know, OK?"

"Sure, Dad. Thanks."

"What's that album you're listening to?"

"I borrowed it from Chris," Mark replied, turning the volume back up. "Attila and the Huns."

From the speakers, guttural noises and screeches accompanied by a tom-tom and twangs from electric guitars sallied forth and assaulted my ears.

"Turn that down," I commanded. Mark complied. I picked up the album cover. Five cavemen were gnawing on bones from a human skeleton.

"Attila and the Huns? Next thing you know they'll have 'Adolf and the Hitlers,'" I said disgustedly.

"You mean 'Hitler and the Gas Chambers'? That English punk rock group? They're so gross. Where did you hear about them, Dad?"

"The English have a group named after Hitler, after what he did to them?" I asked incredulously.

Mark shrugged. "What did he do to them?"

"Are you serious? Don't you know who Hitler was?"

"Some German guy, wasn't he?" he said uncertainly.

"Didn't you even watch *Holocaust?* Or did it conflict with *Laverne and Shirley?*"

Mark lay back down on his bed and stared at the ceiling. I felt a little bit ashamed.

"I'm sorry, Mark. I guess you guys haven't studied World War II in school yet. Here," I said, walking over to the bookshelf and pulling out a dog-eared copy of *Rise and Fall of the Third Reich.* "If you're interested, this book will tell you all you need to know about Hitler."

Mark looked at the thick book with the same enthusiasm

he displayed when asked to take out the garbage. He took the book and set it on the floor.

"I guess I'm just not a World War II nut like you and Matt," he explained.

"Mark, please don't put Matt's books on the floor."

"Oh. Sorry."

"And get on that book report."

"I'll get right to it," he assured me. As usual, he didn't put up any fight. But as I shut the door, I saw him lie back on his bed, and as I climbed the stairs, I heard the stereo blast forth again.

"Mark, turn that off and get on that report!"

The noise immediately stopped.

Sometimes talking to that guy was like punching a pillow. You got no resistance, but you knew you were making no impression.

Chapter Two

The Great Anticlimax, commonly called Christmas Day, was like most other Christmases I've survived. We got up at five-thirty to peals of excited laughter. After the gifts were opened, some of the kids asked accusingly, "Is this *all?*" There were some bickering and fighting because a few of them had been too excited to sleep much and had gotten up too early. At nine-thirty I sent the offenders to bed and made them stay there till noon. Once again there was peace on earth.

We were determined to make this a memorable Christmas, realizing that this would be the last time for quite a while that we would all be together. Matthew was going to the Missionary Training Center in two weeks, Mark would leave before he got home, and by the time Mark returned, Matt and Brenda would probably be married and might be living far away.

In the afternoon, we drove to my brother Ryan's house in Salt Lake. We were all tired late Christmas night by the time we got home, and I had just entered that delicious stage between dream and wakefulness when the ringing of the telephone jerked me back into consciousness.

Attorneys, doctors, and bishops get lots of calls at odd hours. Bishops and attorneys should never be called late at night unless it's an absolute emergency. But doctors charge such high fees that their consciences won't let them sleep anyway, so it's OK to call them anytime.

"John? This is Kurt Vanderhoft. Did I wake you up?"

"No, I had to get up to answer the telephone."

"Listen, we've got a couple of suspects in the county jail that we'd like to interrogate. Can you come over?"

I groaned inwardly. I disliked criminal law. When the judge took all the county legal aid cases away from me, I had consoled myself with the thought that I no longer had to handle criminal defense cases either. "Kurt, you know as well as I do that the judge isn't going to appoint me to defend either of them. Why don't you call one of the judge's favorites and ask him?"

"The rest of them are either not home or not sober. It's important, John. I wouldn't get you out of bed if it weren't. And the judge approves. Would you please come over?"

"OK, I guess so. Give me ten minutes." I hung up and got dressed. We didn't have much crime in the county, and I didn't like getting out of bed to go hold the hand of someone who had celebrated too much by punching out his mother-in-law. Sanpete County did have a major robbery once, and we're proud of it. I think we've had a burglary too—so we can hold our heads up because we're like other places.

The county jail and sheriff's office are in the basement of the courthouse in Manti. I'd never seen it crowded before. But that night, besides the entire sheriff's department, the Ammon city police force was in attendance. With Ammon Police Chief Heber Reitzen and Officer Ed Alvirez, I noticed a new officer. From Mark's accurate description of his mass, I recognized him as Officer Frost, the man who had given the boys a hard time about their hair.

"Where's the county attorney, Ed?" I asked.

He pointed to a door. "Kurt's in there with the sheriff."

"What's this all about?" I inquired.

"There was a robbery and shooting at the dry cleaners here tonight. Three people were killed."

"Two people were killed," Chief Reitzen corrected. "The third one is still alive. Has a bullet in her head, though. They don't know if she'll make it."

The news startled me. I hadn't expected anything so serious. "Who were they?" I asked with concern.

Ed shook his head. "I didn't recognize any of the names."

"Lexia Wainsgaard was killed. Her daughter Wendy is the one who's still alive, last we heard," Chief Reitzen said. "I don't know the third guy, but his name is Aaron Coombs."

"Names don't sound familiar," I said.

"You haven't lived in the county long enough to remember President Wainsgaard and his wife. He was stake president here about fifteen years ago, before he died. Sister Wainsgaard was heavy-set, in her mid-sixties, owned the dry cleaners. Wendy was short, heavy, kind of retarded, a flat face that looked kind of squashed. She's in her thirties but was still living with her mom."

I shook my head. I still didn't recognize them.

"Sister Wainsgaard worked in costuming for the *Mormon Miracle Pageant*," Chief Reitzen continued.

"Oh, yeah," I said. "Old-style glasses, never stopped talking or smiling?"

He nodded. "Sweetest, most enthusiastic lady you'll ever meet. When the all-points bulletin came out, Officer Frost here recognized the car and arrested them."

At the mention of his name, Officer Frost grinned proudly. With his pear-shaped body, khaki Stetson hat, and close-set, pig-like eyes, he looked like he had stepped out of a Burt Reynolds' movie. All he lacked were reflective glasses and a Southern drawl.

"Good job, Officer," I said.

He shrugged. "It was nothing. Just doing my job," he replied complacently.

I walked past him and knocked on the door. It opened, and I walked in. The room was small and bare, painted a bleak white and furnished only with folding chairs. Kurt Vanderhoft was sitting backward on one, his arms around the back of the chair.

Kurt had been Sanpete County attorney for almost sixteen years. In our county, we don't change things unless there's a good reason for it, and Kurt had never given us reason to vote him out of office. He was an enormous man, six-and-a-half feet tall, with a leonine head set on an obese body. He sported a big shock of grey hair on his head that looked like it had never been combed.

Sheriff Stronberg nodded to me, and I nodded back. He had gotten up to open the door for me, then he returned to his seat.

"Thanks for coming, John," Kurt said. "We got a couple of murder suspects in back. One of them says he has nothing to hide. He's willing to talk to us, and we wanted to talk to him before he changes his mind. This is an open-and-shut case that we have against them, so we want to make sure we follow every formality so that they won't have anything to complain about on appeal."

"What makes it so open-and-shut?" I asked.

"A neighbor saw their car parked outside the Wainsgaard house, and one of the suspects had Aaron Coombs's wallet on him, with blood all over it. And the amount of money they had on them tallied pretty closely with the amount stolen from the Wainsgaards. We'll check the money to see if it's got the Wainsgaards' fingerprints on it. If it does, open-and-shut."

"I'll have to advise them not to talk to you," I said.

"I know. But one of them says he was just a hitchhiker and doesn't know anything about it, so he's got nothing to hide. Of course, that's a bunch of bull, but I'm going to get whatever information out of him that I can before he learns to keep his mouth shut."

They brought one of the suspects in. He was handcuffed and shackled. They don't have many opportunities to use such jewelry in Sanpete County.

I told him that he was under no obligation to talk to these men, that whatever he said could be used against him, and that these men were skilled interrogators. I advised him not to talk to them. But he insisted that he was only a hitchhiker and had nothing to hide. So they proceeded to question him. Kurt was especially good—given enough time I believe he could have gotten the suspect to confess that he had committed suicide. After five minutes, the suspect was hopelessly mired in self-contradictions, and I again advised him against talking to these men. He put his head in his hands and said he wanted to talk to his attorney alone.

Kurt and the sheriff got up and left the room. I sat quietly for a while and watched the prisoner as he fidgeted.

"Let me get this straight," he said at last. "Are you my attorney?"

"Well, for tonight, at least."

"Does that mean you can't squeal on me if I tell you some things?"

"It means that anything you tell me relating to a past crime will be kept confidential. I doubt that I'll be your attorney during the trial, but in the event that I am, I've got to warn you that I won't let my clients commit perjury. So don't tell me one thing now and tell the court something else later."

"You mean that if I confess to you now, I have to confess in court?"

"Not at all. You have the right to keep quiet in court. They can't force you to help them convict you by making you talk. But if you choose to testify, it'd better be the truth."

The kid wanted desperately to talk, so I listened. His name was Bryan Sanchez. He was from West Covina, California, twenty years old, and a junior at UCLA majoring in business. His father was an executive in a big corporation. He said that he had never been in trouble with the law before. And he said that he didn't kill those people.

I replied that three people had been shot that night, and the prosecutor claimed that he had an open-and-shut case against him and his partner. Bryan stood up and would have paced if his shackles had permitted it.

"It was all Russell's fault!" he shouted suddenly. He tried to kick his chair, but his chain wasn't long enough and he nearly pulled his leg out from under himself. I jumped up and steadied him. He sat down again, rubbed his eyes with his hands, and started talking.

He stated that he and Russell Montague, the other suspect, had been acquaintances at UCLA. Russell had invited him to come along for a wild Christmas vacation. They drove up to Las Vegas with a couple of girls Russell knew.

Most of the money they brought was lost on the slots. They abandoned the girls and headed north. Russell had told him that they could get plenty of bread if Bryan knew how to keep his cool. He said that he knew how to make a perfect hit and that they'd never get caught. Bryan was reluctant at first but eventually got caught up in the excitement. When they got to Manti, they saw a light on at the dry cleaners, and not many other places were open that late on Christmas night. They stopped, peered in the windows, and determined that only two women were inside. They knocked on the door. The younger woman opened the door, and they pushed their way inside. Once in the shop, they saw that there was also a man whom they hadn't seen from outside. Russell had a small pistol. He told one woman and the man to lie down on the floor, and Bryan hog-tied the two of them. Bryan said that by this time he had lost all enthusiasm for the heist, but since Russell was armed, he did what he was told to do. They took the money from the cash register, and with the help of the old woman they found some more in a box in a closet. After determining that there were no more valuables to be had, Bryan prepared to leave. But Russell returned to the room where the three people were lying. Bryan heard several gunshots, then watched in horror as a smiling Russell came out carrying a blood-covered wallet that he had taken from the man.

They left, and Russell drove south for several minutes until he came to an old abandoned house, well off the side of the road. He parked, then disappeared into the house for a moment. Bryan said that he had considered driving away and going to find the sheriff while Russell was in the house. But he didn't have the nerve. Russell came back without the pistol.

They made a U-turn and drove north, past Manti again. Russell was so unperturbed that when they drove through Ammon, just a few miles past the scene of the murders, he stopped at the Iceburger and coolly ordered some food. Russell had boasted that this would be the "perfect crime," but they soon found that the police around here were no hicks. Just after leaving the Iceburger, they were pulled over and arrested.

Bryan said that he would never have gone along with Russell if he had known that Russell was going to go that far. Bryan was just after a little excitement. Then he despairingly asked me if I thought he would go to the electric chair.

"We don't have electric chairs in Utah; we have firing squads. I imagine that the county attorney will go for the death penalty. But if what you're telling me is true, you won't get shot."

I then explained that since I probably wouldn't be his trial attorney, I wouldn't discuss strategy, but it seemed to me that he might get a reduced sentence in return for testifying against Russell. However, since the county attorney didn't need his help to get a conviction, he better not get his hopes too high. Sanpete County was not tolerant of criminal behavior. We had recently sent a man to the Utah State Prison for stealing a turkey worth less than twenty bucks. It was successfully argued that the theft was a felony because it fit the felony livestock rustling statute, instead of being a minor misdemeanor. In Sanpete, they mean business, and criminals are advised to steer clear of the area. After that cheery note, I warned Bryan that warm friendly jailers and cellmates were notorious finks, so he should do all his talking to his new attorney. Bryan didn't have anything else to talk about so I called a deputy to take him away.

I walked back into the sheriff's office. Kurt Vanderhoft and a deputy were the only people left in the office. I motioned to Kurt, and he followed me into the hall.

"Kurt, I hope you're going to keep quiet about the bloody wallet and the money. If that gets out prematurely, these guys won't be able to get a fair trial anywhere."

"Don't worry, we're going to keep this under our hats until

the trial. Everybody connected with this has been instructed about that, and we're getting a gag order to put teeth into it."

I leaned back against the wall. "Well! I guess my professional connection with this case is over, thank goodness. This is going to be a rough case. Sometimes it's a blessing to be on the judge's blacklist."

"I'm glad you're not going to be on this case, either," Kurt said quietly. "Defending one of these guys could be fatal when you run for county attorney."

"I wasn't even thinking of that," I said. Having been Sanpete County attorney for almost sixteen years, Kurt felt it was time for a change. He intended to run for state attorney general in the next general election, so he wasn't going to run for county attorney in the coming year. I intended to run in his place and was considered a shoo-in for the spot, especially since I had Kurt's support.

"You ought to think of that," Kurt said. "You could ruin your chances."

"I don't believe that," I replied. "People realize that the accused is entitled to a defense, and that an attorney has to defend a man when a court appoints him to do so."

"You'd be surprised," Kurt countered. "All this talk about 'coddling the criminals' has gotten a lot of people thinking that attorneys will do anything to get their clients off. They watch too much TV, I guess. Most people don't realize the distinction between protecting a man's constitutionally guaranteed rights and 'trying to get him off scot-free.'"

"Kurt, I'm sure most people understand 'innocent until proven guilty.'"

"Only in a vague, theoretical sense. When applied concretely, the public doesn't think much of the maxim. When a crime is committed and a suspect is found, the public wants blood. They want to see someone punished, and they figure that the cops wouldn't arrest the suspect unless he were guilty. And they figure that if an attorney defends that suspect, the attorney approves of whatever the suspect did and will try everything to get him released."

"Well, the problem is academic for me anyway because Judge Hastings won't appoint me to the case."

"I've wondered about that," Kurt remarked. "What on earth did you do to get her so riled at you?"

I told him how the feud had started. Two years ago I had helped my neighbor, Helen Olsen, go after her ex-husband to collect on some badly overdue child support. He was constantly in arrears, even though he had lots of bucks. With the help of Nick Hansen, another local attorney, Mr. Olsen had been fairly successful at hiding his assets.

Judge Hastings had just been appointed to the bench. I asked her to find Mr. Olsen in contempt of court for refusing to obey the court's support orders. I wanted her to throw him in jail evenings and on weekends until he coughed up the bucks. Mr. Olsen would still have been able to keep his job, but he wouldn't have been able to have much fun. It was a good technique for enforcing child support obligations. Considering Mr. Olsen's chronic delinquencies, the previous judge would have thrown him in the slammer. But at the time, Judge Hastings was a little insecure about her new powers. Maybe I protested too much—I have a tendency to get more than mildly upset when a father with money forces his children to live in poverty. Judge Hastings warned me to be quiet. When she refused to jail Mr. Olsen, I quietly groaned in disgust. She got angry and said, "You want contempt of court? You got contempt of court!" She then fined me fifty dollars. She had not appointed me to any cases since then, which put a financial strain on me. The court-appointed cases, both civil and criminal, were given to Nick Hansen, who in my opinion was as qualified to practice law as a hog butcher is to perform open-heart surgery.

"Does that hurt you in court, having the judge sore at you?"

I smiled. "If anything, I think she leans over backward to make sure her personal dislike of me doesn't affect her professional judgment."

"Maybe I ought to get her mad at me."

"Shouldn't be hard," I replied. "Well, it's late. I'm going home."

It was a clear, cold night. City lights always dim the stars, and when I was growing up in Salt Lake, we could see only the brightest ones. But in Sanpete valley the night sky is a vast expanse of celestial lights. Usually I couldn't look at a starry sky without thinking divine thoughts. But that night, as I gazed at the heavens, I was wickedly grateful that I didn't have to get involved in that wretched case.

Chapter Three

News travels fast in a county of our size, and it wasn't long before the community became aware of the fact that two of its members had been murdered. Special editions of the *Ephraim Enterprise, Manti Messenger,* and *Ammon Advocate* were on our porch by midmorning with most of the details. The murders quickly became the chief topic of conversation in the county.

I was in my private office just before quitting time when Mrs. Henderson buzzed the intercom and told me that a lady wanted to talk to me.

"Send her in," I replied.

The woman who entered looked familiar, but I couldn't quite place her. I motioned to her to sit down.

"What can I do for you?" I inquired pleasantly.

"Mr. Lindsey, will you keep quiet about the things I'm going to tell you?" she asked nervously.

I nodded my head. "I'm not allowed to discuss my client's confidences."

"My name is Roxanne Springhurst. I'm a nurse at the Gunnison Hospital."

I recognized her now. I often went to the hospitals in Mount Pleasant and Gunnison to visit sick members of our ward.

"A little while ago, I was assisting in surgery. When the doctor finished, I counted the sponges and found there was one missing. I guess I should've counted them before the doctor started to close, but I forgot. I told the doctor about the missing sponge, but instead of reopening, he just yelled at me, 'Well, I didn't leave any inside!' He didn't even order an X-ray to check if there was one inside. I just need to know if I can be sued for any of this."

"You say that it was your duty to count the sponges before he finished?"

She nodded. "But I told the doctor about it as soon as I remembered to count them. But he wouldn't do anything about it."

"Is it dangerous for a sponge to be left inside?"

She nodded again. "It'll eventually start to decay. If it's still in there, like I think, that poor lady is going to have trouble down the road."

"An X-ray would definitely show whether it's there?"

"The sponges have steel fibers in them so that they'll show up."

"Now, do you work for the hospital or the doctor?"

"The hospital. The doctor isn't on the hospital staff."

"If the patient ever sues, you and the doctor and the hospital will probably all be named in the suit. But the doctor was in charge and left the sponge in, so he would probably be held liable, especially since you told him of the problem when he could still have easily corrected it. He had the power to rectify the problem, and you didn't. Legally, you'd probably be in the clear."

"Thank you," she said. She got up to leave.

"Wait a minute, Mrs. Springhurst."

"Oh, your bill?"

"No. What about the patient?"

"What do you mean?"

"Aren't you going to do anything about the sponge?"

"Hey now, I did my part—I told the doctor. It's his business now. Don't worry, when she starts feeling bad, the doctor will order an X-ray and find the sponge. If it's the same doctor, he probably won't tell her what's in there; he'll just tell her that it's a complication from the last surgery. But he'll go in and get it."

"Sit down, please," I requested. She did so.

"Mrs. Springhurst, when that sponge starts decaying and the patient starts suffering, the damage will be done. You've said that it's dangerous."

"Well, it could be. But I'm sure he'll get it in time."

"You can't just let that patient suffer."

"Now look, Mr. Lindsey. If that doctor is too bullheaded to do anything about it, that's his problem. I told him—it's on him now."

"What if she dies?"

"Oh, come off it. She'll start hurting before she dies."

I shook my head in disbelief. "Don't you feel an obligation? Especially since you made the mistake in the first place."

"I have three kids and an ex-husband who isn't too conscientious about his support payments. One of my kids is starting college next year. I've got a good job with seniority, but I could get fired for my part in this. Not to mention the fact that doctors stick together and they'd make it tough on me if I squeal on this guy. Now, just make sure I'm not liable and send me the bill."

"We are talking about a human being here," I replied. "We're talking moral obligations, not legal responsibility. That patient is going to be endangered and her health damaged if you keep your mouth shut. Don't you nurses take the Hippocratic Oath?"

She shook her head a little reluctantly. "We repeated something or other when we graduated, but it wasn't the Hippocratic Oath."

"Mrs. Springhurst, you have an obligation to fulfill. I don't know who this patient is. I don't know the doctor. Something has to be done to keep an innocent patient from suffering. We don't want her to have to pay for another operation that was due to something you and the doctor did wrong."

"She's insured," she replied, as if insurance companies had inexhaustible funds.

I clenched my fists. "Now look! Someone's going to suffer because of you. By the time she starts noticing, the damage will be done. I can't believe you could be so calloused. You and I and everyone else have a moral duty to correct the ills of society as much as it's in our power to do so. But what you're doing is contributing to those ills, and you don't seem to care. You just can't put the whole thing on the doctor's shoulders and deny any personal responsibility."

She looked uncomfortable. I rarely lectured a client, but I continued.

"What you ought to do is tell the doctor, and if he still refuses to do anything, tell the hospital administration. They'll probably be defendants in any lawsuit about this, so they'll do something."

"If I do that, I might lose my job," she said miserably.

An idea occured to me. "Look, why don't you tell me the doctor's name, and I'll handle it?"

"He'll know who turned him in."

"He'll have no way of knowing it was you. I'll send him a letter on my legal stationary hinting that I know about the situation, warning him to cure the problem, and promising dire consequences if he tries to retaliate on anyone. He'll be too scared to take it out on anybody."

"You won't mention my name?"

"Not if you don't want me to," I assured her. "Who's the doctor?"

"You swear you won't mention my name, no matter what?"

"I promise."

"Dr. Durkess," she said.

I didn't recognize the name. "Then he's not a Sanpete doctor?"

She shook her head. She borrowed one of my phone books and found his address for me, then got up to leave.

"How much are you going to charge me for this?" she asked.

"Unless we have to pursue this matter further, not a cent. Thank you for doing the right thing. You've really helped your patient a lot."

"You'd just better not tell on me," she warned.

"I won't. Thank you."

As I escorted her from my private office and through the waiting room, I was somewhat surprised to see Mark lounging on the couch across from Mrs. Henderson's desk. He asked me if he could walk with me to the church after I closed. We helped Mrs. Henderson into her car, locked up the office, and walked down the street together through the gathering dusk.

Until Mark took that fateful aptitude test as a sophomore, he had almost invariably shown up at my office at quitting time to walk home with me. Sometimes we talked about things that were on his mind, but most often we just quietly enjoyed each other's company. However, after the test, as my exhortations for him to get on the ball became sharper, his appearances at my office became fewer, until they ceased altogether.

"Dad," Mark said at last, breaking the silence, "how could those people do that?"

"You mean the murderers?"

He shook his head. "How could the Germans do what they did to the Jews and the gypsies and the Jehovah's Witnesses and the Slavs?"

"Have you been reading that book?" I asked with some surprise.

He nodded. "But I still don't understand how people could do stuff like that to other people."

"If I knew the answer, I'd tell you," I admitted. "It seems that the Germans had been trained that obedience was the big thing—rigid conformance to rules and laws seemed to permeate them. They didn't question the orders of their lawful superiors. They felt that any moral blame for their actions was borne by their superiors. At the Nuremberg trials, I'm sure you remember reading the comment the defendants made over and over, 'I was just obeying orders.'"

"But crud, Dad, those extermination squads that just went

around murdering people, how could they do that? How could they line people up and shoot them or march them into the gas chambers like that? The Germans were Christians, weren't they? They had the Bible and the Ten Commandments. They must have known that what they were doing was wrong."

"I imagine that at first they must have felt that something was wrong," I replied. "But things like consciences can be perverted. The more you disregard your conscience, the less it speaks. 'The Spirit of God will not always strive with man,'" I quoted. "The Germans were eventually able to talk themselves into believing that they were doing the right thing."

"Dad, you always used to say that if one righteous man had the courage to step forward against evil, the righteous majority would follow him. Didn't anyone try to stop the Nazis?"

"Not very hard, I guess, not while they were winning. I don't pretend to understand it myself. But I've got several more books on the subject. Maybe they'll help."

"No thanks, Dad, it makes me sick," he replied. We fell back into silence for the rest of our walk.

People in cars and on foot were converging on the church as we got closer. Mark and I found ourselves walking with President and Sister Tuttle, and Mark gallantly offered to carry the large covered roasting pan that President Tuttle was carrying. President Reuben Tuttle was the second counselor in the stake presidency.

"How are things going, Reuben?" I asked.

He shook his head. "I don't know. The assistant regional director of the BLM is retiring in May, and I was informed today that they'll give me his job if I want it."

"Hey, that's great!"

He shrugged. "It's a big step up for me, but it'll mean relocation in Denver. I've spent my whole life in this county, and I just don't know if I want to leave. But Barbara is from Boulder, and she's eager to go so she can be closer to her family."

"We've lived by your family for twenty-five years, so it's only fair that we live by my family for a while," Sister Tuttle countered.

I grinned. "If Barbara is as persuasive as Carol is, I suspect that next May, we'll be waving good-bye."

President Tuttle nodded his head ruefully, and Sister Tuttle smiled in triumph.

As we walked down the sidewalk in front of the church, a passing car honked its horn and pulled over. "Bishop Lindsey!" the driver called. "Can I talk to you for a few minutes?" It was Moroni Fitzgerald, our stake president, who exercised ecclesiastical authority over the twelve wards in Manti, Ephraim, Sterling, and Ammon.

"Certainly, President," I replied. He parked his car in the church parking lot and held the church door open for Mark, the Tuttles, and me. He chatted warmly with Mark for a few minutes, then the President and I went into my office.

He asked me about the welfare of myself, my wife, and each child. With him, it wasn't merely perfunctory. The man really cared, and I always felt love and warmth flow from him. Then he settled himself into a chair and pulled a pen out of his pocket. He had an unconscious habit of playing with his pen whenever he got down to business.

"John, you know that in two weeks we'll be here for your annual ward conference."

I nodded.

"You know that you've served for over five years as bishop, and we don't usually ask a man to serve more than five years."

I nodded again. I had been expecting this, with both a sense of regret and relief.

"John, would you have any objections to continuing as bishop for a while?"

This was a surprise. "No, it's fine with me," I replied.

"Well, John, I felt like it was time to release you, but the Lord said no. I don't know why. So if it's OK with you, we'll ask you to continue until the Lord says otherwise. You don't have any ulcers yet, do you?" he asked with a slight smile.

I shook my head.

"You can always tell how good a bishop is by looking at his pants and seeing if they're worn out at the knees or at the seat," he continued. "I've noticed that your pants wear out at the knees. At the risk of sowing seeds of pride in your heart, I want to tell you that you're doing an outstanding job, Bishop."

My ears turned red with embarrassed pleasure. Though we are supposed to seek approval from the Lord and not from men, it was nevertheless gratifying to hear that my efforts were appreciated.

There was a light knock on my door, and my daughter Brenda stuck her head in. "Oh, sorry, Dad," she said when she saw President Fitzgerald. "We didn't realize you were busy."

"Just leaving, Brenda." He smiled as he rose and bid us goodbye. My numerous progeny pushed past him into my office.

It's because of people like me that the Planned Parenthood Association has declared Utah a disaster area. My oldest son, Matthew, was born about nine months after my marriage. Brenda followed ten-and-a-half months later, and with a speed and determination uncharacteristic of his later years, Mark showed up less than eleven months after that. Fortunately for the physical health of their mother and the mental health of their father, Paul, Cindy, Susie, and John Jacob IV made their appearances at reasonable intervals. Ten months after John IV's death, John Joseph was born.

I accompanied my children to the cultural hall, which was beginning to fill with people. This was our ward's "Christmas Leftovers Dinner," a brainchild of my wife when she was serving as Relief Society president several years before. Tired of preparing meals from Christmas dinner leftovers, she made a bunch of phone calls and within half an hour had organized an informal potluck get-together to use them up. The idea caught on and became a ward tradition. But like some traditions, it eventually became self-defeating: in order to ensure plenty of food for the Leftovers Dinner, members cooked up so much extra food that we ended up eating leftovers from the Leftovers Dinner. But the tradition continued; ours was an extremely sociable ward, and the members looked forward to any excuse to get together. They were good people, and at the risk of sounding sentimental, I have to say that I love them.

As I walked around, shaking hands and exchanging pleasantries, I noticed that this was a subdued group. The news of the murders had thrown a pall over the festivities. Most of the members had known the Wainsgaards and the Coombses, and some of them had been very close to the victims.

However, things livened up somewhat when the Kanagawa family arrived. They were offering samples of Japanese delicacies to anyone who had the nerve to eat them. I sauntered over and several people urged me to eat something. I calmly picked up an octopus tentacle, a piece of raw fish, some whole dried minnows, and some squid. I munched them all down, while on-lookers gagged.

Sister Kanagawa was wearing a beautiful silk kimono that no longer fit her very well. Her youngest son, Mike, was dressed in a cotton kimono he had bought when he was a missionary in Japan.

"Bishop, how does that little tape recorder you had me buy for you work?" Mike asked me.

"Pretty good," I replied. I had sent Mike some money to buy me a tiny Japanese tape recorder that was smaller than a cigarette pack. "Of course, it's got the tone quality of a tin can," I added, and he laughed.

"Where's your husband?" I asked Sister Kanagawa.

She pointed. "Sitting over there, like a stick-in-the-mud."

I looked over to where Tom Kanagawa was sitting. I have to admit that when I first moved to Ammon, I felt a tightness in my stomach when I first saw Brother Kanagawa.

During my early childhood, Mom was remarkably free of prejudices, and my older brothers and sisters grew up relatively untainted. But then came the war. My father was an engineer and general contractor. When his business slackened during the depression, he went to work for a big construction firm engaged in government work. When Congress belatedly saw war clouds approaching and appropriated money to develop bases in the Pacific, my father's firm was hired to help build an airfield on Wake Island. My father was one of some eleven hundred civilian workers who were on Wake with the five hundred Marine defenders when the Japanese attacked. When Wake fell the day before Christmas Eve, my father was interned. All of the surviving Marines and most of the civilian workmen were shipped off to spend the rest of the war in prison camps, but my father was one of a hundred American workmen kept on the island to finish the airstrip. On October 7, 1943, the Japanese marched my father and the other workmen down to the beach and machine-gunned them.

I cried when the war ended and we were informed of my father's death. But in a way I think that my sorrow was borrowed from the other members of my family, since I had only the vaguest memories of my father. I was far more affected by the change in my mother. Unlike the rest of us, she didn't cry; instead, she hardened herself. For many years, she never wept and rarely smiled, and one of the things I learned at her knee was to hate the Japanese.

Mom had a compartmentalized mind: she could maintain an intense hatred of the Japanese and yet pity the innocent Japanese-Americans who had been put into concentration camps in Utah and other western states. But such mental gymnastics were too much to ask of a small child, and I found myself unjustly hating everything connected with Japan, however remotely. The prejudices learned as a child are tough to overcome, and even though I began to realize in my late teens that my blanket hatred of all things Japanese was irrational, that didn't make it any easier to rid myself of it. Several months in Okinawa while I was in the Marine Corps helped a lot, for knowledge is the antithesis of prejudice.

But, when I moved to Ammon and saw Brother Kanagawa sitting on the stand at sacrament meeting, I still felt that automatic gut reaction. I tried hard to overcome it, and I believe I succeeded. It was easier with Sister Kanagawa and her kids, because they were extroverts and popular in the community. But

Tom Kanagawa was different. He was a proud, aloof man, who never spoke unless spoken to. He operated a successful vegetable farm and plant nursery in Ammon. He and I eventually became friends of sorts, but the only things he seemed willing to discuss were the Church and gardening. Since I have a love for gardening, I won his respect. Someone had told me that Tom had been a hero during World War II. Being a military man and an amateur historian, I enjoyed war stories but could never get Tom to talk about his war experiences.

I sat down by Brother Kanagawa.

"Hi, Tom. Why aren't you over there gorging yourself on octopus and squid?"

Brother Kanagawa laughed. "It makes me sick. You seem to be doing OK, though."

"I was just showing off. I ate the stuff in Okinawa. Octopus and sushi are pretty good. That squid tastes like a piece of old innertube, though."

Tom agreed that octopus was all right. "But I'd prefer a Big Mac anyday."

"Did you really have all that stuff for dinner yesterday?" I inquired.

Tom smiled. "No, we had turkey and pumpkin pie. Mike decided to cause a sensation, so he bought all of that from an Oriental store in Provo."

I sat there awkwardly for a minute. I always had trouble thinking of things to say to him. Fortunately he broke the silence.

"How'd your blackberries end up? Did you ever figure out what disease they had?"

"Naw, never did," I replied. "Only about a third of the berries ripened, and the rest just rotted on the vine. Those stupid blackberries seem to catch every disease that comes along, and I never get anywhere near the crop I expect. It's such a pain keeping them trained onto the wires, too. I got so sick and tired of fussing with them that after I harvested what was left of the crop, I went out with a shovel and wiped out the whole patch."

Brother Kanagawa looked at me as if I'd just told him that I'd sacrificed my firstborn to Moloch. "You wiped out your blackberry patch? All those plants? I can't believe it!"

"I'm sorry now that I did," I admitted. "I mean, I love the fruit—blackberries are my favorite—but in a way I'm also glad that I don't have to fuss with them anymore."

Tom shook his head. "You didn't get rid of them, John. The only way you get rid of blackberries is to sterilize the ground. Those berries will be back. Once you've got them, you're stuck with them. It's true, they seem to pick up every bad thing that comes along. And if you don't train them right and keep a close eye on them, they'll go wild on you. Maybe you don't always get the fruit out of them that you expect, but if you handle them right, the fruit you get is the best stuff in the world." He shook his head again. "You wait, you haven't gotten rid of them."

We sat in silence for a minute, watching Mike trying to coax one of our elderly matrons into eating an octopus tentacle.

"That's pretty good delegation of authority, getting your wife and boy to do it all," I said with a smile.

"Well, heck, I don't know anything about Japan," Tom replied. "I've never been there, and I don't speak Japanese. I hate the food, and my wife and kids tell me I don't even pronounce my last name properly."

"Was your wife born in Japan?"

"No, she was born in Los Angeles, just like me. But her folks sent her back to Japan to go to high school."

"Born in California, huh? How did you end up here?"

He turned his head and gazed at nothing. I wondered if he hadn't heard my question.

"What brought you to Utah, Tom?" I repeated.

He turned his head slowly and looked at me. "The United States government."

"Oh, you were in the service here?"

He stared at me for a moment before replying. "No, in the concentration camp."

"The concentration camp?"

"I assume that, being a lawyer, you've heard of the *Nisei* concentration camps," he said sardonically.

I felt somewhat flustered, as if I had unintentionally probed too deep. "Well, yeah, sure, a little bit. I heard Senator Hayakawa talking about it a while ago, saying how the Japanese-Americans shouldn't be bitter and just to forget it."

"Bitter? Heck, I'm not bitter. Just because the government locked up my whole family without benefit of trial, why should I be bitter? Just because they imprisoned natural-born American citizens without charging us with any crimes or giving us any of the rights guaranteed by the constitution, what reason do I have to be bitter?"

"I heard they did it for your own protection."

He laughed. "Just like they protected old James Wakasa. Comes to a little fence, tries to climb it, and the sentry blows him away. For his own protection, of course. Or my mom, who grew up in southern California and suddenly gets thrown into a tarpaper shack in the frigid Utah climate. She died of pneumonia. But I'm sure it was for her own protection."

"Well, what about the spies and saboteurs?"

"During the entire war there was *never* an act of sabotage or espionage committed by a single person of Japanese ancestry. When things got tense between us and the Japanese, three government agencies, including the FBI, investigated us *Nisei* and unanimously agreed that we were loyal to the U.S. We were no threat at all.

"But we had bought a lot of poor land and built it up into prime farmland. The *Nisei*'s land in California alone was valued at a quarter of a billion dollars—in 1942 dollars. That's quite a hunk of bread. The war gave Californians the perfect opportunity to take it. The people screamed that we were a security risk, and Roosevelt moved us out. Dad was smart. He put a bunch of cash in a trust to pay the taxes while we were in the camps. But that didn't save us. In 1943 California passed an escheat law—confiscated it all, even though we were paying the taxes. Sold it and made a bundle."

"But I heard the government paid you back after the war," I said.

"Yes, they distributed thirty million dollars. I'm not much of a mathematician, but I see a discrepancy between thirty million and a quarter billion. Most of us never got a cent. What they paid out was just conscience money—made the public feel better. They could tell themselves that our country is a land of justice for all. Equal rights for all.

"But heck," he continued, "I got nothing to be bitter about. Mom died of pneumonia in the camps, Dad died a drunk migrant worker after the war, and they buried my brother in Italy, after they'd drafted him to fight for a country that had taken everything away from us. But, like Senator Hayakawa says, I have no right to be bitter."

I hesitated for a moment, then said, "I heard you were a war hero."

He looked at me but didn't reply.

"Did you serve?" I persevered.

He sighed. "Yeah, I served. Left a foot and three fingers in Europe." He held up his right hand, which had only a thumb and little finger on it. I had known about his injury, but he would never tell how it had happened.

"Were you decorated?" I asked.

He nodded his head briefly.

"What did they give you?"

He looked away, then mumbled, "D.S.C., with an oak leaf cluster."

The Distinguished Service Cross. Second only to the Congressional Medal of Honor. And he had won it twice.

Chapter Four

I was sitting in the county courthouse's tiny law library a few days after the dinner when the door opened behind me.

"John?"

"Oh, hi, Martha." It was Judge Hastings's secretary.

"Your secretary said you were here. Are you busy? The judge would like to talk to you."

I shut my book and walked down the hall to the judge's chambers. I knocked on her door and was told to come in.

Judge Hastings was seated at her desk. She wasn't in her judge's robes; she was dressed in a plain brown pantsuit. To paraphrase Isaiah, she had no form or comeliness; there was no beauty that we should desire her.

The judge was not popular in the county. Some felt that she should have been home taking care of her kids instead of presiding at court. But most people disliked her for her attitude. She was regarded as opinionated and egotistical. It was popularly supposed that she had her eye on an appointment to the Utah Supreme Court. Though I pretty much agreed with the county's evaluation of her personality, if I were the governor I'd put her on the Supreme Court. Once she had overcome her initial insecurities, she became a very good judge. She combined an ability to keep her personal feelings from coloring her judgments, with the knack of tailoring the law to fit the needs of justice. I was glad to practice law before her, though I did my best to keep out of her way outside of court.

"Shut the door," she commanded. I complied.

"Mr. Lindsey, I know you're a bishop. I suppose that means that you knew Lexia Wainsgaard and her daughter."

I shook my head. "I've seen them around. But I wasn't acquainted with them personally. Her husband was stake president several years before I moved here."

She looked surprised and rather pleased. "I understand that you've worked on a murder case before."

I nodded. I suddenly caught the drift of her questioning, and I didn't like it. I answered cautiously, "Well, I've sort of worked on one before."

"What do you mean, 'sort of'?"

"When I was working for a firm in Salt Lake, they were handling a murder defense. But I was low man on the totem pole, and my only involvement was a bunch of research. I didn't do any of the trial work."

"Research is often the most important part of a case," she said firmly. She leaned back in her chair and regarded me for a while. She had enormous eye sockets, reminding me of a chameleon. She leaned forward again and put her elbows on her desk.

"Mr. Lindsey, I'll get to the point. I want you to defend one of those two murder suspects. Russell Montague. This morning I sent him to the state mental hospital for observation. He just sits and stares, never talks. Unless you have some valid reason for declining, I'm appointing you as his counsel."

My reaction would have made Clarence Darrow ashamed of me. She hadn't assigned a case to me for two years. My finances had taken a beating because of it. And now here she was trying to foist off on me a criminal case that could be a real nightmare. "I thought Nick Hansen was taking this case," I said.

The judge's face turned dark and angry. For reasons unfathomable to the attorneys of our district, Nick Hansen appeared to be the judge's pet. Some thought it was political—they were both Democrats—but I thought that it was simpler than that: they had both come to the valley about the same time, so they were both the "new kids on the block." But the judge's favor for Hansen did not extend to the courtroom. In her official capacity, she was fair and impartial.

The judge picked up a paper clip and proceeded to mutilate it.

"Listen," she said angrily, "that jerk Hansen came in here this morning after the preliminary hearing and said he had to be dropped from the case. Said his involvement in this case would hurt his chances at getting elected county attorney!"

She threw the mangled paper clip into the wastebasket with a shot that would have made Danny Ainge proud.

I shared the judge's anger at Hansen. According to the canon of ethics which all attorneys are supposed to uphold, an attorney may not refuse a court appointment to defend a man simply because he believes the man is guilty, he finds the case repugnant, he is afraid of offending the community, or he fears losing business by associating himself with the case. Refusing a case for political reasons was a definite violation of the ethical canon.

The nasty thought occurred to me that she was assigning me to this case to hurt my chances and enhance Hansen's, but I dismissed it from my mind. Whatever her character flaws might be, I didn't believe they extended to using the bench to influence politics.

"To tell you the truth," she said, "from the first, I've had qualms about using Hansen in an important case. He just isn't qualified to handle something like this. We can't have any mistakes in this trial. The whole state is going to be watching. Everyone's performance has to be flawless. Hansen's too sloppy—I'd trust him with an uncontested divorce or a DUI, but not this. But that doesn't excuse his wanting to get off for political reasons."

She picked up another paper clip and bent it all out of shape. I wondered distractedly how much money the state shelled out each year to keep her in paper clips. She again threw the disfigured clip toward the wastebasket but missed. She looked at me meaningfully. I walked over, picked up the paper clip, and threw it into the wastebasket.

"Mr. Lindsey, I recognize that this is not a pretty case. I

didn't know the Wainsgaards or Mr. Coon either," she said, mispronouncing his name. "But I'm shocked and sickened at a senseless murder like this. What I want to know is, are you enough of a professional to put aside your personal feelings and give this man the kind of representation that the Constitution entitles him to have?"

I didn't want this case. No one would want it. I had no sympathy for the perpetrators of this crime, but they were entitled to trained counsel to make sure that if they were convicted, it was all done in accordance with the law. Life was full of unpleasant duties. I didn't like performing them, but I wasn't much good at shirking. "I can handle it," I said reluctantly.

"You don't have to sound so enthusiastic," she said. "You look like a jackass eating cactus. Hates it, but needs it to stay alive."

That was a fair description of how I felt.

Another paper clip was systematically destroyed and joined its fellows in the plastic graveyard.

"Look, I've assigned Brent Crenshaw to defend the other suspect . . ."

"Do you think it would be better for me to take Bryan Sanchez?" I interrupted. "I've already talked to him about the case." He'd be a lot easier to defend, I thought. Plead guilty and testify for the state, getting a reduced sentence. The kid hadn't fully realized what he was getting into.

She shook her head. "Take Montague. As I was saying, I've assigned Brent Crenshaw to defend Sanchez. For heaven's sake, don't let him turn this trial into a circus!"

I smiled a little. Brent Crenshaw was a relatively young attorney, who graduated high in his class and was considered to be very creative. Sometimes he was so creative as to be ridiculous. A few years ago, Brent had a client who had gotten inebriated and defaced several campaign posters of Jimmy Carter. He was arrested and charged with vandalism and public intoxication—little offenses with small fines. But a fit came on Brent, and he climbed up on his Constitutional high horse. He urged his client to plead not guilty. Brent argued in court that his client's act had been nothing less than a political statement, the most protected form of freedom of speech. It ended up costing his client hundreds of dollars in attorney's fees and court costs. Brent was outraged at the guilty verdict and would have fought to his client's last dollar to protect his Constitutional right to free speech. But his client had already been sufficiently embarrassed and impoverished, so when Brent wanted to appeal it to the Utah Supreme Court, his client told him to drop dead. However, during Brent's sane periods, he was a very good attorney indeed.

I promised Judge Hastings that I would keep an eye on Brent, then left. She scored another basket with her paper clip as I walked out.

As I went past the county attorney's office, Kurt hailed me and told me to come in. "What was on the judge's mind?" he asked as he shut the door behind us.

I sat down on the top of Kurt's desk and proceeded to mutilate a paper clip. The habit was catching. "She's assigned me to defend Russell Montague."

He shook his head. "I was afraid of that."

"I don't mind," I lied. I would have to repent that night.

"I know she's been having a tough time finding suitable attorneys," Kurt said. "Seems like most of the attorneys in six counties claim they were the Wainsgaard's best friends or neighbors or relatives. Some of those who didn't even know the Wainsgaards found other excuses. It's a rotten case, John. Looks like you're the only guy around here that couldn't think of an excuse to offer the judge, so you got stuck with the dirty work. Hey, did she take Hansen off the case, or is he assisting you, or what?"

"He's off."

He chuckled grimly. "Well, John, he's sure done you in— the judge is using her power to keep you out of office and put Hansen in."

"I don't believe that, Kurt."

"Do you know if he asked off, or did she sack him?"

I didn't reply.

"Attorneys have been disbarred for refusing to accept an appointment."

I still didn't say anything.

"Well, what the heck. You want a Coke to drown your sorrows?"

"Got a Sprite?"

He opened his tiny refrigerator and got us both drinks.

"This case is going to be rough on you next election," Kurt stated. "Whey you're running for county attorney or attorney general, you've got to yell 'Law and Order!' as loud as you can and talk about putting an end to criminal coddling. Come next November, people won't understand why you defended this guy."

"Kurt, we've been over this before. I've got a reputation in this county. I'm not brave, so if someone asks me why I'm defending this guy, I'll tell them it's because the judge appointed me. People can understand that."

Kurt shrugged. "It's your neck."

"Well, there's no honest way out, so I'll do my job and you do yours. I understand my client was sent to Provo for a mental evaluation," I said to change the subject.

"Yeah. He's acting like a real fruitcake. Like they say, 'Honesty is the best policy, but insanity is a better defense.' The shrinks will tell us whether or not he's faking."

"I can handle a murder defense, but I've never been involved in an insanity plea. Where do you look for all the bleeding-heart shrinks?"

"Don't worry," Kurt said. "I can point you in the right direction. I had an insanity case once. Won, too."

That surprised me. In spite of all the publicity such cases get, insanity defenses are very rare, and a successful insanity defense even rarer. "When was that?" I asked.

"When I was practicing in Reno. About twenty years ago. My client had shot his neighbor. My client was kind of a dizzy-looking guy, but just as nice as he could be. I asked him what happened. He says, 'Well, Mister Vanderhoft, I was out pheasant hunting. Didn't hit a darn bird all day. When I came home, I saw my neighbor across the street working on his roof. It was just too good a shot to pass up.'"

"And you won?"

Kurt finished his Coke, crushed the can with a powerful grip, and threw it into a box in the corner. "Yeah, we won. A cakewalk. Even the state's psychiatrists agreed that the guy was nuts. But my client spent the rest of his life in the loony bin."

"Will you show me what you've got on my client?"

"Sure. Hansen's got some of it. I'll have my secretary run off a copy of everything I got. You can pick it up in an hour or so." Kurt was one of those enlightened prosecutors who believed that the defendant and his counsel had a right to know everything the state had against him. In some jurisdictions, the prosecutors are really tight with their information, forcing the defendant to file discovery motions and do lots of expensive investigation. It doesn't make much sense, especially when the defendant is indigent and the state has to foot the bill for his defense. In return, Kurt asked the defense not to pull any dirty tricks.

"Uh, John?" Kurt said quietly. "You could always get your client to fire you. Make him mad, insult him, tell him what you think of him. That'd get you off the hook."

"Knock it off, Kurt. I'll be OK. As long as justice is done, the people in this county won't care who's representing these guys."

"I think you're naive, but I hope you're right."

I crumpled up the empty can and dropped it in the wastebasket. Kurt bent down and fished the can from the wastebasket and threw it into the box in the corner. "The Cub Scouts asked me to save my cans for them," he explained. "John, you realize that I'm going to kill you on this case," Kurt said without rancor. "Your client doesn't have a stinking chance. I'm going for the death penalty, and I'll get it too. There won't be any plea bargaining. So, I want you to fight like all get out for those guys. We don't want them to be able to argue on appeal that they had incompetent counsel. Of course, with you representing them instead of Hansen, I don't need to worry about that."

"I'll protect every right my client has," I said evenly.

An hour later, Kurt's secretary brought me copies of the evidence he had against my client. As I looked through it, I had to agree with Kurt. My client didn't have a stinking chance.

Chapter Five

On New Year's Eve, we said good-bye to one year and welcomed in another. The next day I groggily helped Brenda load her things into my pickup, then drove her back to her apartment near BYU. Like a patient beast of burden, I unloaded her suitcases and boxes while Brenda cooked me a deep-dish apple pie in appreciation. Then I hit the road, continuing north on the Interstate.

Cottonwood is an unincorporated suburb on the east side of Salt Lake Valley, a few miles south of the Holladay suburb where I grew up. I drove my pickup down lanes bordered by forests of trees. The houses were well back from the road, hidden behind the timber. I turned at a sign that said "Private Lane—No Trespassers" and continued down the forbidden path. I drove through a gate that had been left unlocked in anticipation of my visit and parked on a circular driveway. I caught a glimpse of the swimming pool and tennis court as I walked up the stairs and rang the doorbell. I decided that I was in the wrong profession. A lovely young woman answered the door.

"Hello, is Dr. Avalon here?"

She looked at me doubtfully and gazed past me at my pickup. I was regretting having come in Levi's and a denim jacket, but I hadn't wanted to get my suit dirty while hauling Brenda's belongings.

"May I ask who's calling?"

"John Lindsey."

"Oh!" She smiled and pushed a button on the intercom. "Dad, that lawyer's here."

A few moments later, Doctor Avalon appeared. He was somewhat taller than I, with an athletic build a little slimmer than my own. To have a daughter as old as the one who answered the door, he must have been several years older than I, but he didn't look it. His face was unlined, and his brown hair had not a trace of gray in it. I attributed it to Grecian Formula 16. Like his daughter, he gazed past me at my pickup. He looked at me as if wondering whether I had interrupted my slopping of the hogs to come see him.

"Come in."

I entered. When he made no effort to shut the door, I shut it.

"Doctor, thank you for seeing me on a holiday. Saved me from having to make an extra trip."

He shrugged deprecatingly. He indicated for me to follow him. I followed him off the marble-floored entry and down the oak-parquet floor of the hallway. He stopped outside a door, motioned for me to go in, and shut the door behind us.

The room smelled like a freshly cleaned stable. There were leather sofas next to the walls, with cowhide rugs on the floor. Leather-bound volumes lined the bookshelves. I wondered if he owned a tannery.

I sat in one of the leather chairs and sank uncomfortably deep. He sat behind a big desk and clasped his hands in front of him.

"What can you tell me about my client's mental condition?" I asked.

"What do you know about psychiatry, counselor?"

I shrugged. "Not much. I took a night course once in psychology, about marriage counseling."

"Well, then you don't know anything about psychiatry," he stated. That was certainly a pleasant icebreaker. I wanted to ask him what he knew about procedural due process, but I refrained.

"In your medical opinion, is my client insane?" I asked.

"*Insane* is not a medical term, it's a legal term," he replied.

"OK, then in legal terms, by the standards of the ALI rule, is my client insane?"

"The ALI rule is woefully inadequate, counselor."

I sighed. Why was he being so difficult? "Nevertheless, it is the law in this jurisdiction and many others. So tell me, is my client insane by the laws of Utah?"

"No."

"Thank you."

"You're welcome."

We fell silent for a moment. I looked at his bookshelves. I hadn't been aware that *Love Story* and *Valley of the Dolls* were available in leather-bound editions.

"So, does my client have any mental problems?"

"Tell me, counselor, do you know what a psychopath is?"

"I dunno. A guy who goes around foaming at the mouth and gets his jollies from cutting people up, I guess."

"You're wrong, counselor."

"Tell me, doctor. Why are you so friendly to attorneys? When you were young, did your mother beat you with a copy of *Black's Law Dictionary?*"

He tried hard to keep from smiling. Finally, he quit fighting it.

"I'm sorry," he said. "I have to admit that I have some deep-seated negative feelings about lawyers, even though I have to work with them occasionally. Then when you showed up dressed like Little Abner, I decided that it was your way of showing contempt for me and my profession. And to tell you the truth, I've been feeling out of sorts ever since I started evaluating your client."

"You were reading too much into my behavior," I said. "We hicks always dress like this. Actually, this is my formal outfit—what I wear for weddings and court appearances and stuff like that. If this were informal, I wouldn't have worn my shoes."

"OK."

"Now, tell me about my client, doctor. You say his behavior disturbs you?"

He leaned back in his leather swivel chair. "Mr. Montague apparently must have taken a basic psychology course. He's faking symptoms of catatonic schizophrenia. Not doing a very good job of it. I eventually got him talking though. I was sorry I did. It's hard to shut the guy up."

"But he is sane, then."

He leaned forward and put his hands on the glass top of his desk. He tried to erase a smudge on his desktop with his thumb, but only made it worse. "By the M'Naghten rule, he's sane," he replied. "He was aware of the nature of the act he was doing, and he knew that the act he was committing was wrong. Or at least, not accepted by society. By the ALI standards he's sane. He suffers from no mental defect that keeps him from appreciating the wrongfulness of his conduct or conforming his conduct to the requirements of the law. He does have a bad case of grandiose delusions, but delusions of grandeur do not make an insanity defense."

"So my client is normal?"

"I didn't say that. Your client displays all the classic symptoms of a psychopath."

"But you said he's sane."

"A psychopath is not a foaming-at-the-mouth mass murderer. A psychopath is not even necessarily a criminal. For some reason, psychopaths are usually extremely intelligent but incapable of giving or receiving love. They lack a conscience and feel no remorse. They have a tendency to use other people to help them with their depredations, and then they turn on their accomplices and throw them to the wolves. They have an utter contempt for authority, and they fear no punishment. Rehabilitation is just about out of the question. Like I say, they aren't necessarily criminals, but because of their talents, they make good criminals. And great lawyers."

"So my client is a sane psychopath?"

"He is sane, by the standards of the legal profession, yes."
He leaned back in his chair. "I recall one study I read about.
They hooked up a psychopath to some monitors and told him
that at noon he would receive some severe electrical shocks.
When they do that experiment with normal people, their anxiety level goes up. As noon approaches, the normal subject is in
agony, fearing the shocks that he thinks are coming. But you
know, the psychopath didn't feel a single tremor. Psychopaths
don't like punishment, but the thought of future punishment
doesn't bother them. Or deter them."

"You said that they're intelligent?" I asked. That seemed
doubtful to me, in view of Montague's stupid blunders that
ended in his easy capture.

"Yes, but they also have an utter contempt for authority.
For example, Montague is extremely intelligent, but he figured
that the authorities were so stupid that they'd never catch him.
So he sat around in Ammon and ate burgers instead of getting
while the getting was good."

"If he's told you the whole story, he must really enjoy talking."

"The man loves to talk—you'll get sick of him. He's
strange, has a lot of strange ideas and a unique philosophy. For
example, he believes that evil will ultimately triumph over
good, and he gets quite superstitious and silly when he's talking. I've never met anyone like him before. I'd love to take him
apart and see what makes him tick. He's incredibly melodramatic too. I guess you'll have to talk to him to find out."

"How did he become a psychopath? Was he born that way,
or was it his parents' fault, or what?" I asked.

He rested his head on the back of his chair. "Who did sin,
that this man was born blind?" He shook his head. "There're
plenty of theories, but they don't matter. I hate to be rude, but
I'm missing the Cotton Bowl. Do you have any more specific
questions about your client?"

"Do the doctors at the state hospital know that my client is
a psychopath?"

"They'll know that he's faking his catatonic schizophrenia. About his psychopathy, I don't know, but I doubt it. It depends on how much he talks to them, and I hear he's keeping quiet around them."

"Well, thank you for your time, Doctor. I appreciate your willingness to see me on a holiday like today." I arose, and he escorted me to the front door.

"Uh, Mr. Lindsey, my wife tells me that I take people too seriously. Can I assume that you were joking about wearing that outfit in court?"

"Yeah. I didn't wear my suit because I was helping my daughter move into an apartment so she could start back to school tomorrow."

"Here at the U?" he asked idly.

"No, down at the Y."

"Oh?" He looked surprised. "Are you a Mormon?"

"Yes."

"I guess you're not . . . what's the word they use? Active?"

"I try," I replied. "Some people in my neighborhood would say that I'm active. Why?"

He looked at me quizzically. "How can you do what you're doing if you believe what you believe? I'm agnostic, yet I have trouble sleeping sometimes when I get involved in cases like this."

It would take an hour's answer, or none at all. "Doctor, you're missing the Cotton Bowl," I said dryly. I turned and briskly walked away.

Chapter Six

Montague, my client, kept up his charade about being crazy. He must have realized that it was his only way out. I visited him at the state mental hospital in Provo, but he acted like a zombie all the time I was there. I wondered how Dr. Avalon had gotten him to talk. I told him that I knew he was faking and that I couldn't very well prepare a defense without him. But he continued to stare straight ahead, playacting to the end. During the thirty days of observation, I visited him a few more times with no better results.

In the meantime, I tried to prepare a defense for him without his help. Working on his defense was like digging holes and filling them in again. It was clear that no amount of effort would make any difference in this case, but I had to do the footwork anyway.

Adney Cannest was Ammon's real estate broker. His real estate office was on Main Street right across the road from his home. He and I used to be really close. We had both served in the bishopric with Bishop Meers, Adney as first counselor and I as second counselor. To my surprise (and, no doubt, to the surprise of everyone else) I was called to be the new bishop. I wanted Adney to be my first counselor, but the Lord disapproved. The deterioration in Adney's and my relationship seemed to date from that time. He became somewhat distant and was full of hurtful jibes disguised as humor. My wife, who reads a lot of psychology books and is fond of practicing without a license, said that she believed that Adney wanted to be the bishop. I don't know. St. Paul wrote, "If a man desire the office of a bishop, he desireth a good work." Change the "good" to "lot of," and you'll be closer to the facts. But the intangible rewards more than compensate for the sacrifices.

Adney was a good man, honest and hardworking both in his business and Church work. Only one incident marred my opinion of him.

Members of the bishopric interview the young men and women in the ward quite frequently. Several years ago, when Adney was first counselor, he interviewed Matt. At Sunday dinner that afternoon, Matt reported that in the interview Adney had said, "God judges a man differently in his business dealings than He does in his personal life. There're certain things you have to do in business to keep ahead." I was incensed. I replied that God makes no such distinctions, that if a man finds he can't compete in business without compromising his honesty, he ought to change professions. It disturbed me to hear that an authority figure like Adney would teach something like that to my son. In the LDS Church, people are disfellowshipped or excommunicated for shady business dealings.

But it was puzzling. In the time I had known Adney, I had never heard of him doing anything that did not correspond to the highest ethics of his profession. Everyone I knew that bought or sold through Adney, including myself, had felt fairly and honestly treated. He had a good reputation, and as a result, he had a thriving business, even in the current slump.

Adney was at his desk meditating with his eyes closed when I walked into his office. The tinkling of the bells on the door woke him up, and he stretched. He didn't take his feet off his desk.

"Oh, hi, Bish," he said. "How's my favorite liar, I mean lawyer?" He laughed—I grinned because I was supposed to.

"Oh, Bish, did you hear the latest? This old farmer was in a graveyard, looking at the tombstones. He comes to this one tombstone that says, 'Here lies a lawyer and an honest man.' He scratches his head and says, 'Seems like an awful small grave for two men.' "

I laughed. That one was funny.

"How're things going?" I asked.

"Rotten. This recession is killing the real estate business. I only netted fifty-six grand this year. I should have become a lawyer like you."

I don't know why he was telling me how much he made, since I already knew from tithing settlement a few weeks before. He probably correctly suspected that he made more than twice as much in the past year as I had.

"Well, what brings you here?" he asked.

"I understand that you were present when my client was arrested. I just wanted to hear what happened."

Adney leaned back in his chair. "I've already talked to the police, the sheriff, and the county attorney. Why don't you get it from them?"

"I did. But I'm trying to be thorough. I just want to make sure we didn't miss anything."

His face hardened. "Trying to find some technicality to get them off with?"

"No."

"Bishop, lots of us find it hard to swallow that you're defending these murderers. I was a stake clerk under President Wainsgaard. He and his wife were the nicest folks you'll ever meet. And now here you are, a bishop, trying to get Lexia's murderers off. Kind of bothers us to realize that lawyers don't care who they hurt or how many criminals go free, that they're more concerned with winning than with justice. More concerned with the rights of the criminals than with the rights of the victim. Instead of punishing criminals, the law does everything it can to find some way to let them go."

The anger in his voice didn't bother me. "You've been reading too many issues of *Reader's Digest*," I replied. "The criminal justice system does have its problems, but in spite of what you hear, it does a good job of separating out the innocent and punishing the guilty. I don't blame the media. They do a real service by pointing out the problems so they can be corrected. But they do give the wrong impression of a pretty good system."

"What about all those criminals being let loose because the police did some little thing that might have violated their rights?" Adney complained.

"You're talking about the exclusionary rule. You're misinformed. When officers violate a suspect's rights, they don't automatically let him go. If they've seized some evidence illegally, they can't use that evidence against the suspect in court, but they can use anything else. Even in that famous Miranda case, where all that 'You have the right to remain silent' stuff came from, they didn't let the fellow go, even though his rights had been violated. They gave him a new trial with no violations of rights and convicted the fellow again. The only reason you hear so much about cases like that is because they're so rare. The media thrives on the unusual. It happens, but not all that much."

"It's still not right for even one criminal to get off just because of what some cop did. Why punish society just because of some lousy cop?"

"The police are representatives of the state," I explained. "It is the responsibility of the state to set a good example. It is not a prerogative of the state to enforce the law by breaking the law. Some police were abusing their power, so the courts fashioned safeguards to curb those abuses but still enable the police to operate effectively when they stayed within the legitimate limits of their powers. In spite of what you hear, those safeguards don't really hamper the police to a great extent. It does help to keep the bad apples on the police force in line."

"You're sure full of answers today," Adney said, unconvinced. "But I still don't understand how a guy like you can defend a murderer and try to get him off."

"I'm not trying to get him off. I was appointed by the court to defend this man. I don't have much of a choice. But when I say that I'm defending this man, it doesn't mean that I approve of what he's accused of or that I'm defending his right to do what he's accused of. In our country, a man is innocent of a crime until he is proven guilty beyond a reasonable doubt. It is the duty of the state to prove that my client is guilty beyond a reasonable doubt. It is my duty to *force* the state to prove that my client is guilty beyond a reasonable doubt. I am to check the believability of the state's evidence, the legality of its methods, and the competency and veracity of its witnesses. In other words, it is not my duty to get my client off, but it is my duty to make sure that if my client is convicted, he is convicted legally, in accordance with the rules of the law. I'm sort of a legal watchdog. I will not get my client off any way I can. I will not lie or permit others to lie. I will not present evidence that I know to be untrue. What it boils down to is this: I obey the law by making sure that the state obeys its own laws. Obeying the law is my duty. 'We believe in being subject to kings, presidents, rulers, and magistrates, in obeying, honoring, and sustaining the law.' 'Let no man break the laws of the land, for he that keepeth the laws of God hath no need to break the laws of the land. Wherefore, be subject to the powers that be, until he reigns whose right it is reign.'"

The appeal to Church doctrine softened Adney a little. "Well, gee, it still seems that all this stuff is too formal and strict. Everybody knows these guys are guilty. The cops wouldn't waste their time arresting these guys and keeping them locked up if they were innocent. So why don't we eliminate all this legal gobbledygook and punish them?"

"Tom Kanagawa and 120,000 others were locked up for three years in spite of the fact that they were innocent," I replied. "That wouldn't have happened if they had been granted the 'legal gobbledygook' of a formal trial to protect their constitutional rights as citizens. A formal trial allows all the evidence, both pro and con, to be presented in an orderly manner. The evidence will be tested before a neutral, unprejudiced group of people. After all the evidence is in, they will determine if the state has proven beyond a reasonable doubt that the guy is guilty. That doesn't mean 'beyond a shadow of a doubt.' Just a reasonable doubt. We don't want a man to be deprived of his life if substantial doubt remains as to his guilt."

Adney didn't say anything. He still looked a little dubious.

"Adney, let me bore you with a personal experience. Back in the olden days, I was quite a nice little kid, even if I say so myself. Smart, polite and respectful. So naturally, I was the teacher's pet. Mrs. Hart was my school teacher. When we found out about my father's death after the war, Mrs. Hart made an extra effort to be nice to me. She and I were really close.

"One afternoon Mr. Simon, our principal, came into our room with this little kid. He told Mrs. Hart that at recess for the past several days, somebody would sneak up behind this little kid and give him a hard chop on the neck, then run away. It had gotten to the point where the kid's parents couldn't get him to come to school. He was so scared he'd throw up every time his parents tried to make him go. When they found out why, they told the principal. Mr. Simon was bringing him in to see if the kid could find the guy who was hitting him. The problem was, the kid had never seen the guy's face, since he always attacked from behind and was running away before the kid could turn around. All the kid was sure of was that his attacker had black hair and was wearing a red coat. I sat there innocent and un-worried—I mean, there were two other black-haired boys in our class and dozens in the whole school, and I knew I was in-nocent. When Mrs. Hart heard this kid's story, her face turned red. She marched to the back of the room where our coats were hanging, and she picked up my coat. She brought it up and stood in front of me. She said, 'This is your coat, isn't it, Johnny?'

"I nodded, but any fool could see that it was maroon; not red, but kind of a dark reddish-purple. So I still wasn't worried. But then Mrs. Hart said, 'We've found your culprit.' Mr. Simon grabbed me by the scruff of the neck and started to bounce my head against his stomach. He was saying things like, 'A bully, huh? Like to pick on little kids, huh? Attacking from behind, huh?' Well, naturally I was crying, but between sobs I said I didn't do it. So the principal hauled me over face to face with the kid and asked him if I were the one who was hitting him. The kid shrugged. He'd never seen his attacker's face. The principal yelled, 'Well, you said he had black hair, and you said he had sort of a red coat, and this coat is sort of reddish.' Notice that the kid hadn't said that the coat was sort of reddish, he had said it was red. The principal was changing the facts to fit the evidence at hand.

"Rather than argue with the principal, the kid first said that I was probably the one. After the principal badgered him some more, the kid became certain that I was the culprit. Mr. Simon was a short-tempered overreactor, and he started to drag me from the room by the neck, saying that his school had no room for a kid like me. But Mrs. Hart stopped him. She asked him to let her take care of it herself. She told him that my dad had just been killed, and she was sure that that was the reason I had suddenly become a bully. Another amateur shrink. But the principal relented. At the time war orphans had a special place in society, and most people were willing to make allowances. So he left. Mrs. Hart kept me after school and told me how ashamed of me she was. I continued to maintain my innocence. That made her mad. She felt that confession was the first step toward repentance, and she wasn't going to settle for anything less than a full confession and a wholehearted turn around. Denying my guilt would only make it worse, she said, so I wouldn't get recess or lunch periods or any privileges until I acknowledged my guilt. Maybe I would have been better off if I had confessed to something I didn't do.

"Before, Mrs. Hart had been warm and loving to me, and now she was cold. I did a little checking around, and I found that the class next to ours had two black-haired kids, one with a plain red coat and the other with a red plaid coat. I told Mrs. Hart, but it just made her angrier. Ours was the first class the principal had visited, but a suspect had been found, so the search was ended. Mrs. Hart wouldn't even investigate further.

And as if to confirm my guilt, after they kept me in for recess, the kid wasn't hit on the neck anymore. That satisfied Mrs. Hart. But shucks, the whole story was around the school by then about how they had got me, and naturally the real culprit would lay low when he found out that the principal was after whoever was hitting the kid.

"I think I know now why Mrs. Hart refused to check out the other two boys, and why she wanted a confession from me so badly. She had judged and punished me, and if it were later discovered that the wrong child had been punished, she would have felt awful for being so quick to condemn me. If she could coerce a confession from me, it would justify my punishment. She wasn't a bad lady. She was good, and she had been one of my favorite teachers. But she was human. Humans jump to conclusions. When a crime is committed, they grab the first plausible suspect and fasten the guilt on him. Until the Supreme Court fashioned safeguards, it wasn't unusual for police to torture confessions from suspects. It's easier to torture a suspect into an untrue confession than to keep looking for other suspects, and a confession justifies the torture and pacifies the conscience of the torturer.

"In my case, because I refused to acknowledge my guilt, I spent the rest of the school year at my desk with no recesses. It was unfair, and I guess I made it worse by striking back. I went into civil disobedience. I wasn't a discipline problem—I merely sat at my desk and read books. I wouldn't answer questions or look up or even acknowledge Mrs. Hart's existence. My reputation as a bully and a troublemaker carried on through my elementary years, though I never did anything to justify it.

"My wife says that I forgive but that I never forget that I forgave. I guess that's true. Mrs. Hart made life miserable for a nice little boy, who desperately needed her affection, not her scorn. After more than thirty years, it still hurts when I think about it. Mrs. Hart is dead now. On Judgment Day, I'm going to tell her again in front of the heavenly hosts that I didn't do it."

We were quiet for a moment.

"Why didn't your folks do anything?" Adney asked softly.

"Mom had just received word that she was a widow. Her second son was in a hospital fighting for life after being burned in Okinawa by a flamethrower. Her oldest daughter was about to jeopardize her eternal salvation by marrying a gentile. Mom had enough things to worry about. The minor school troubles of her youngest child were of no great consequence to her."

"Is that when you decided to become a lawyer?"

I smiled a little. "No, that's when I decided to become a Marine so I could shoot everyone who'd been mean to me.

"Anyway, Adney, that's my sob story. It's typical of human behavior. That's why our justice system exists: to permit reasoned judgments based on real evidence instead of snap judgments based on assumptions and prejudices. Sound reasonable?"

"Yeah, I guess so." He sounded like he was convinced against his will.

"Will you do me a favor, Adney?"

"What?"

"Next time you hear people questioning my motives for defending this guy, will you tell them what I told you? I'm human. I want to be understood and liked just like everybody else."

"If I can remember it."

I got out my tiny tape recorder and recorded his recollections of the arrest. I left, hoping that in spite of whatever doubts Adney had concerning me, he would defend me from local talk. In the next few months, I would need defenders.

Chapter Seven

After thirty days of observation, Russell Montague was pronounced clean by those high priests of American society, the psychiatrists. Instead of being returned to the county jail at Manti, he was sent to the larger and more secure facilities at Richfield.

I had spent a lot of time in Richfield in my youth. I'd lived there with my father's relatives while Mom rushed through college to get her teaching degree. To me, Richfield was always the Valley of the Hicks. I don't know why I felt that way. Richfield is bigger than Ephraim, Manti, and Ammon put together, yet I never think of them as hicksvilles. Perhaps it's because Ephraim has the college to educate it, Manti has the temple to sanctify it, and the blessings of both overlap into Ammon.

I am related by blood or marriage to perhaps five hundred of Richfield's inhabitants. My Richfield relatives are the kindest, most hardworking, and most Christian group of people in the world. Also the most boring.

One of my reasons for settling in Ammon was to be close enough to my Richfield relatives to handle their legal affairs and attend family gatherings, yet far enough away to prevent them from casually dropping in. Financially, my scheme was a failure. They never get arrested, they work out their differences with their neighbors, and they turn the other cheek when necessary. Exasperating people like them can ruin a lawyer. They've always been good to me, though. They're proud of me because I'm the first Lindsey to earn a doctorate and one of the few to serve as a bishop.

I pulled into a parking lot at the Richfield jail the morning Montague was taken there. I told a deputy sheriff who I was, and he led me inside the jail and down a corridor.

"Rick," the deputy said, "Montague's lawyer's here to see him."

I recognized the jailor immediately as a relative of some sort. I'd seen him at reunions, but I had to think a minute before I could place him.

"Aren't you married to one of Clarissa Wilson's daughters?" I asked.

He grinned. "Yeah, sure am. I'm Melissa's husband. You're the emcee at the reunions who tells all the doctor jokes, aren't you? Lessee, Johnny, isn't it? What's your last name?" he asked as he offered his hand.

"Lindsey, John Lindsey."

"Oh, you're actually a Lindsey? I always thought it was strange how at the J. J. Lindsey family reunions there weren't many people actually named Lindsey. What relationship are you to J. J.?"

"J. J. was my grandfather. In fact, I'm the bearer of the family name. J. J.'s full name was John Jacob Lindsey, Senior."

"How can you be his grandchild? Clarissa's older than you are, I'm sure, but I think J. J. was her great-great-grandfather."

"Well, you see, I'm the last child of his last son, so that tends to telescope the generations. J. J. died before I was born. Even most of his kids are dead now. But I'm only two generations removed from him. It all depends on birth order."

"I guess that makes sense. So you're Montague's lawyer, huh? I thought they'd certified him fit to stand trial. But ever since he's come he's just sat there like a deaf-mute. How are we supposed to feed him?"

The psychiatrists had torn Montague's insanity defense to shreds, but it sounded like Montague was going to carry on his masquerade to the end. I waited in a little room while Rick went to get Montague. When Rick came back and brought Montague in, he was acting like a zombie. Rick seated Montague, then left.

"Well, Russell, how are they treating you?"

He silently stared into space like a stone Buddha.

"Russell, it's no good. You've been under psychiatric observation for thirty days, and the shrinks say you're faking it. Those are neutral shrinks. And Dr. Avalon, who's on our side, says that you're faking it too. If you can't even fool your own side, you may as well give up."

He still said nothing.

"Well, I'm leaving," I said, picking up my coat. "Took me nearly an hour to get here, it'll take another hour back, so I'm not going to waste any more time on you. When you want to talk to me and help prepare your defense, call me. Until then, just remember that in Utah we shoot people. You're charged with a capital crime. If you won't offer any assistance in your defense, I guarantee that you'll be convicted, and when the appeals end, they're going to take you to a special room at the prison and blow you away. Good-bye."

"Hey, wait!"

I came back in and shut the door. "Well, the stone Buddha speaks."

I sat down.

"What do you need to know?"

"I need to hear your version of the events. Let me check them out. Then we'll see where we stand."

"What evidence do they have against me?"

"Not a lot," I replied, "but what they have is devastating. A woman claims she saw a dark green Mustang parked next door to the dry cleaners about the time the murders took place. You were driving a dark green Mustang when you were apprehended. And they found Aaron Coombs's bloody wallet in your pocket. Not to mention $340 in cash, most of which had the Wainsgaards' fingerprints on it. In your favor is the fact that no murder weapon was found on you. They've searched thoroughly between the place of the murder and the place you were arrested. But the prosecutor will claim that you threw it out the window when you saw the cop's lights and somebody picked it up and didn't report it."

Montague stood up and paced.

"Before you say anything, Russell, let me tell you some things. Anything you tell me will be kept in confidence by me. I couldn't talk if I wanted to, and if I did talk, the court would be required to throw it out. On the other hand, I won't suborn perjury. If you try lying in court, even in your own defense, I'll stop the proceedings, demand to be excused from the case, and leave you high and dry."

"So you're saying I have to confess?"

"No, but you don't have to testify. You also have the right to fire me at any time. I think if you look, you might be able to find some attorney who'll let you lie your head off."

Montague continued pacing. He stopped in a corner and gave the wall a sharp kick with his foot.

"How about a plea bargain?" he asked. "I'll agree to testify against Sanchez in return for a few years in the clink."

"I imagine that's what Sanchez will do to you."

"Well, let's do it to him first."

"You're forgetting that the money and wallet were found on you, not on Sanchez."

Montague thought for a moment. "He forced me to put them in my pocket. He had the gun and said that if I didn't put them in my pocket, he'd kill me too."

"Sounds nice, but I imagine that if he testifies, he's going to tell where the gun was hidden. A fingerprint test will tend to show who handled the gun."

He thought again for a moment. "After he killed those people and made me put the wallet and money in my pocket, he got a cloth and wiped off his fingerprints from the gun, then made me take the gun. I had nothing to do with the whole thing."

"The prosecutor's going to ask you why you continued to

do as Sanchez told you after he handed you the gun. If you had the gun, Sanchez couldn't make you do anything. Plus the fact that Sanchez has never been in trouble with the law before. He's an excellent student—"

"So was I!" Montague interrupted. "I was straight A all the way!"

"Yes, with two drug-peddling offenses that were plea bargained down."

"That's not supposed to be on my record! When I turned twenty-five, I thought they were supposed to wipe out stuff like that from your record."

"For certain purposes, the Youthful Offender's Act does clean your slate. But it doesn't totally wipe out your record, no. The prosecutor will tend to believe Sanchez because of his clean record. Plus you've sort of hurt your credibility by pretending to be loony."

He paced around for a few more minutes. From what Dr. Avalon had said, I had thought that Montague would feel no anxiety. But perhaps I'd misunderstood him, because Montague sure looked spooked to me.

"How about if I plea bargain to second-degree murder? Think they'd accept that? Twenty years or so in the clink?"

"Russell, the county attorney wants to parade your head on a stick down Main Street. He's planning to run for attorney general, and you've given him the ticket. This will get his name before the voters. He's already said that he'll go for the death penalty all the way."

"That's against the law!" he protested. "He's using me to get ahead! Can't you get me off for something like that, if the prosecutor has it in for me?"

"Just doing his job, Russell. The fact that doing his job will also further his ambitions is just gravy for him. He does have the responsibility to prosecute you to the furthest extent of the law."

Montague plopped down on his chair. He put his head in his hands. He finally lifted his head and asked, "What do you suggest?"

"Russell, I've talked to every witness, read all the reports, seen all the prosecution's evidence, and I haven't been able to come up with a thing. I'll go through everything again, but unless I can find something, I'd say they have you."

"Why don't we plead insanity?"

"Because you're not insane."

"I'll fake it."

"No you won't. I'm an officer of the court, and I will not permit the court to be lied to or defrauded."

He looked at me incredulously. "A million lawyers in the country, and I get the only one who isn't a crook!"

"Russell, no conscientious attorney would let you lie to the court. Even if you could find an attorney with no scruples, you'd lose an insanity plea. Insanity is an affirmative defense. That means that if you plead it, you have to prove it. You can't prove that you're insane. Besides, it's bad tactics. The prosecution can't call up any psychiatrists to testify unless we do it first. Do you really want the prosecution's psychiatrists on the stand testifying that you're a psychopath who ought to be put to death like any mad dog?"

"Can't we plead guilty, throw ourselves on the mercy of the court?" he asked.

"You have to make that decision. You can plead guilty, but your case has a trial phase and a penalty phase. You would be pleading guilty to the trial phase. In the penalty phase, the judge would weigh the mitigating factors against the aggravating factors and decide whether you were worthy of the death penalty. In return for a guilty plea, some prosecutors would refrain from bringing in the aggravating factors, so the judge could only weigh the mitigating factors. The chances would be good, though not certain, for life imprisonment instead of the death penalty.

"I'd rather die than spend the rest of my life in prison," he interrupted.

"That can be arranged," I replied. "The prosecutor here wants your hide. So you could plead guilty and still get the death penalty because Kurt won't arrange any deals. Rumors say that Judge Hastings wants an appointment to the Supreme Court. If she doesn't give you the death penalty, she might look like a criminal coddler. I don't know much about judicial politics, but a death sentence might be better for her career. Of course, that's just idle speculation on my part."

"You're a wonderful defense attorney," he said sarcastically.

"I didn't create the situation. You're welcome to fire me, but you won't get anything better from anyone else. I may not glitter, but I'm thorough."

Montague folded his arms. He stretched out his legs and gazed at the ceiling. "This sure shoots my plans," he said.

"What plans are those?"

"You'd just laugh if I told you. The shrink at the hospital laughed."

"Then don't tell me," I said.

"I wanted to take over the world."

He was right. I rubbed my chin and mouth with my hand to try to cover my mirth. "That's a pretty ambitious project," I said finally, when I could trust myself to speak.

"You probably think I'm just spouting off. But I have the brains and guts to do it. Pretty soon I was going to start."

I recalled that Dr. Avalon had mentioned his delusions of grandeur. "How were you going to go about it?" I asked.

Montague got vague. "I was planning to go into politics. Or maybe start my own religion. A man with brains and guts who's ruthless enough to do anything can go as far as he wants."

"Until he's stopped," I added.

"That's the beauty of it," he said, a smile starting to animate his face. "You see, I can hide behind the law when I need to. That's the advantage evil has over good. Good makes the rules, so good has to keep the rules or else it ceases to be good. But evil can break all the rules it wants to, then hide behind them. Look at the Mafia. Look at the politicians. So evil is going to win in the end."

This guy's records said that he was a philosophy major in college. His philosophy sounded rather sophomoric.

"Good luck," I said.

"You don't believe me, do you? Are you one of these Bible-beating, hallelujah-shouting, born-again Christians who think that the Lord'll come down from heaven to rescue the good guys and punish the bad?" he asked mockingly.

"I'm a member of The Church of Jesus Christ of Latter-day Saints."

"A Mormon, huh? Tempe was lousy with Mormons. Are you active?"

"I'm a bishop."

He laughed. "A bishop! Doesn't it make your skin crawl to associate with a guy like me?"

"I get paid for it."

"Well, Bishop, I guess you believe in all that garbage about how things'll keep getting worse, and finally, just when evil is about to triumph, the Lord makes His grand entrance, and all the wicked are barbequed, and everything is wonderful. I heard that junk from our preacher all the time. Then when I was a teenager, I was over at the house of a guy I knew. His dad had been in the Philippines during World War II, on Bataan. He was telling us how they fought against the Japanese for a long time. MacArthur kept telling them that help was on the way, but it wasn't so. Roosevelt had written them off. They kept telling the soldiers that help was on the way so that they'd keep fighting. And it worked. They kept fighting until they were over-run.

"Well, after I heard that story, the next time my mom dragged me off to church, the preacher was up there talking about Armageddon and Gog and Magog and how the Lord would show up at the last moment to save the day. And it occurred to me that it was all empty talk. Just like the Philippines. No help was going to arrive. God was just telling the good people about an ultimate victory to keep them fighting until they get overrun. You see, there was a battle in heaven, and the devil and a third of his angels lost and were thrown out. But he's gathering up reinforcements here on earth. You have to admit

that there're a lot more bad people than good people. As soon
as Satan has enough people, he'll fight the battle for heaven
again, and this time we'll win!"

Montague's theories were insignificant when compared to
my actual knowledge. His philosophy interested me only in-
sofar as it displayed his character. I didn't care for what he was
telling me about himself.

"Is the killing of good people like the Wainsgaards and Mr.
Coombs a part of your program for victory?" I asked.

"They got in my way—they could have identified me. Plus
there's the absolute thrill of having complete power over
another and performing the ultimate violation of another soul
by blowing his brains away. But I guess you can't understand
that exquisite delight, since I'm sure a guy like you has never
taken a life before."

"I have," I said.

"Killed someone?"

I nodded.

"When? World War Two?"

I shook my head. "I'm not that old. In Vietnam."

"I wish I had been old enough to go there. From what I
hear, it was a blood feast." He cast a mocking glance at me. "You
don't look like a Vietnam vet. You're supposed to be an al-
coholic or a drug addict, with a lot of divorces and no steady
job. Do you still jump out of bed at night and hit the dirt?"

"I used to, for a while. But that's a common aftereffect of
any war, not just Vietnam. My brothers used to do it after World
War Two. But most of the vets with the big problems were those
who served after 1968, when the protests started at home.
Those of us who were there before '68 didn't seem to develop
nearly as many problems."

"Did you see much action?"

"More than most," I said.

He pointed his finger at my face. "Then you look down real
deep in your heart and remember when you were blowing
those gooks away. I'll bet you can't honestly tell me that you

didn't feel that thrill I was talking about, if you're really honest with yourself."

I thought about it. I recalled a sultry night in '65. We had received intelligence from friendly Vietnamese about a well-hidden trail that was frequented by Viet Cong supply columns that would bring down mortar rounds and rockets with which to pound our positions. I took a squad of my men to teach them the finer points of night ambush. We thickly sowed a section of the trail with Claymore mines, then waited. After midnight, they came—a big column. I waited until they were close, then blew off the Claymores. Some three dozen of the enemy fell immediately from the mines' pellets. Then we opened up with small arms fire. Though we had been heavily outnumbered, we had the priceless advantage of surprise. The results were predictable.

In Vietnam, we didn't have victories, we had body counts. Forty-seven V.C. corpses were loaded into the choppers. They gave me a Bronze Star.

Did I feel any ecstatic thrill as I sent some forty souls to spirit prison? I tried hard to be honest with myself. I had felt strong emotions, certainly, as I squeezed the detonators and then fired my weapon. I guess it would be fashionable to condemn myself and admit that the animal desire to kill was strong within me, covered only with a thin veneer of civilization. But it wasn't true. It's a fact that I felt an urgency to destroy as many of my country's enemies as I could before they vanished into the night, and when it was over, I felt a relief that I had beat the odds and was still alive. But in all honesty, I got no pleasure from killing.

I looked at Montague. "To tell you the truth, Russell, I never did get a kick out of killing people."

"I don't believe you, Bishop. No one is that pure in heart." He leaned toward me with a sneering grin on his face. "And I can tell you this: the pure in heart are not going to inherit the earth. The day isn't far off when me and my buddies take over."

His knowledge of the Beatitudes was as mistaken as his

philosophy, but I didn't bother to correct him. "Russell," I said tiredly, "do you remember where you are? And why I'm here?"

The sneer slowly disappeared. Montague stretched his legs out, folded his arms, and stared at the ceiling.

Walking back to my car, I thought about the way I usually handle my clients. I generally tell them the worst that can happen, the best that can happen, and my estimate of what would probably happen to them. In Russell Montague's case, all three were the same. He was going to face a firing squad.

Chapter Eight

At the courthouse several days later, I dropped in to the county attorney's office to talk to Kurt. He wasn't there, but I got the information I needed from his secretary. She also informed me that there had been a development in the Wainsgaard case. Wendy Wainsgaard, who had been in a coma ever since the night of the shooting, had suddenly come out of her coma. At least, that was the unofficial rumor, but Kurt hadn't been able to confirm it yet. An eyewitness, even a somewhat retarded one, would drive the final nail into Russell Montague's coffin.

While I was talking to the secretary, I heard a voice out in the hallway say, "There he is, in there, sir." A tall man with a big smile walked in holding out his hand.

"Johnny, you old son of a gun! How're you doing?"

I shook the hand held out to me, and found myself talking about old times with a complete stranger.

"All these years, and you haven't changed a bit! Johnny and I are old college buddies," he explained to the secretary. I wondered which college.

We walked out into the hall, and he kept talking. He was dressed as though he couldn't decide whether to go to a rodeo, a mass, or an antiwar demonstration. He had on cowboy boots and denim jeans, held up by a belt with an old peace symbol buckle. His pink shirt was made of some kind of silky material, and the top three buttons were undone, revealing a hairy chest and a big crucifix on a gold-chain necklace. He was carrying a beige trench coat. The top of his head was bald, but he had let the hair on one side of his head grow long so he could comb it over the top of his head. He had a big potbelly and would have appeared even taller if not for his poor, slouchy posture.

I finally broke down and asked him his name. He looked surprised.

"Don't you remember good old Jerry? Jerry Newcarter."

Oh yeah. I remembered. Jerry the Jerk.

He was the cousin of Ron Newcarter, one of my best friends at Olympus High and the University of Utah. As a result, I had to be nice to Jerry. At the U, he had been in one of my math classes, and he had triple dated with Ron and me a few times.

"Oh, yeah, Jerry!" I said with a forced smile. "In Professor Snyder's class, you always used to say how the long side of a right triangle was the hippopotenuse."

"Yeah," Jerry laughed.

"I remember at the Hotel Utah Skyroom, how you loosened the heads of the salt shakers on the tables around us." At first use, the heads had come off, spilling salt all over. The management asked us to leave.

"Yeah," he chortled.

"I especially remember that time you brought the lizard to the homecoming dance."

He exploded with laughter. "Yeah, I was sure a card then, wasn't I?"

He had brought a lizard with him and dropped it in the gown of his date. When it finally got out, he recaptured it and tried to put the lizard down my date's formal. In one of the few acts of violence I have committed outside of Vietnam, I shoved his nose into his face. I noticed with creative pride that, more than two decades later, his nose still had a definite list to starboard.

Jerry was one of those guys who thought he was the life of the party, when in fact he was so obnoxious that no one could stand him. I had tried to befriend Jerry because I saw that he needed help. But I gave up trying to reform him after the lizard episode when my girlfriend dropped me because she said I kept lewd company. She was right—Jerry was filthy minded and enjoyed embarrassing our dates. I don't think he ever understood why I quit associating with him. I never did get my girl back. I was surprised at the intensity of my dislike for him, in spite of all the years that had passed, but I decided not to be rude.

"Well, well, Johnny, I hear you're a big lawyer nowadays. Really come up in the world, haven't you? I remember the time when your family was so hard up that all you had was a beat-up Ford," he said with his typical tact. "And they say you're a bishop now! Hard to believe, after some of the stuff you used to do to the girls!" He gave me a knowing wink.

I didn't know what he was talking about. I was always a good kid, and a gentleman with the girls.

"You married, got kids?" he inquired.

"Seven of them," I replied. "How about you?" I asked, though I couldn't imagine any girl being hard up enough to marry him.

"I was." He shrugged. "A couple of kids, before the nag divorced me. You know how women are."

Yes, I know how women are. They're marvelous. Though I generally disapprove of divorce, I admired Jerry's ex-wife for the good sense she displayed in dumping him.

"Well, Jerry, it's been great talking to you, but I've got to head off to Richfield to talk to a client," I said, shaking his hand. "See you sometime." I started to walk away. With the perseverance of an insurance salesman, Jerry hurriedly stepped in front of me.

"OK, Jerry," I said wearily. "What are you selling?"

"What?" He laughed. "I'm not selling anything. I just wanted to talk with an old buddy for a little while."

"What about?" I asked warily.

"Well, I guess you know that I'm a reporter for the *Tribune,* don't you?"

72

I shook my head.

"Oh, sure you do. You've probably read my by-line. I do feature stories for the *Tribune*."

I shook my head again.

"Sure, like the feature series I did on Gary Gilmore's background, and Robert Redford, and that big piece I did recently about Butch Cassidy," he continued.

"Oh yeah. I read the Butch Cassidy article."

He grinned as broadly as if I had extravagantly praised the article and proclaimed it worthy of the Pulitzer Prize. As a matter of fact, it was quite well written and interesting.

"Well, I'd like to do a piece about Russell Montague, just a few feature articles. Some background stuff, you know. Maybe work it into something bigger if he's executed, who knows? Of course, I'd put you in it. Give you some free advertising."

"Go ahead and write it. I won't stop you."

"Well, I was kinda hoping, since we're old buddies and all, that you'd give me some information."

"Jerry, you ever heard of the term *gag order?*"

He nodded.

"Are you asking your 'old buddy' to go to jail for your benefit?"

He shook his head. "Look, Johnny, I don't need to know any of that top-secret stuff. I just want to know what kind of fellow this guy Montague is."

"He pronounces it *Mon-ta-gue,* with three syllables, not *Mon-tague,*" I corrected. "As in *Romeo and Juliet.*"

"Oh? He's Italian? You think he's associated with the Mob?"

"He's American, and he's not with the Mafia."

"I mean, is he Italian-American?"

"I have no idea, Jerry. He's six foot one, twenty-seven years old, has a medium build, blond hair and blue eyes, a bachelor's degree from Arizona State in philosophy and political science, and is a doctoral candidate at UCLA. He's single and quite good-looking. Without his beard, he looks a little like a young George Peppard. His father's an upper middle-class owner of some Laundromats in Tempe. That's in Arizona," I added.

He had pulled out a small tape recorder. "OK if I tape you?"

"No."

"Listen," he said, edging closer, "these statistics you're giving me aren't the things I'm after. What I want to know is, what is the guy really like?"

"You mean, is he really a murderer?"

"No, not that kind of stuff . . . unless you really want to tell me. I just want to know what kind of a person he is. OK?" He gave me what he probably hoped was a winning smile.

I looked up and down the hall. I confidentially motioned for him to bring his ear close to my mouth. He looked excited and drew near. I looked around again cautiously and finally put my mouth up to his ear.

"I wouldn't want my daughter to marry him," I whispered, then briskly walked away. When I reached the end of the hall, I called back to him, "Don't you dare quote me on that!"

He looked put out.

I walked out to my car and drove to Richfield. My distant cousin's husband buzzed me through the electronically controlled doors, and I entered the jail.

"Howdy, Johnny."

"Hello, Rick."

"Come to see our celebrity again? We don't often get mass murderers in our humble jail. Had a reporter here earlier this morning, asking questions about him."

"Alleged murderer," I corrected. "Was the reporter Jerry Newcarter?"

"I dunno. He was a tall, funny-looking fellow from the *Tribune*."

"That's him. He caught me today too. How is our celebrity behaving himself?"

"He's been just fine since you first came. Doesn't act like a zombie anymore. In fact, if you didn't know what he'd done, you'd think he was a heckuva neat guy."

I hadn't seen that side of Montague.

"Could you go fetch him for me?" I asked.

Rick sauntered down the corridor, let Montague out of his

cell, and walked back with him side by side. He laughed at something Montague said. Suddenly, Montague lunged at him and shoved his thumbnails into the jailor's eyes. Rick went down with a cry of pain. Montague ran toward me. I stepped in his way, and he crashed into me, nearly knocking me over.

"Deputy!" I yelled.

I managed to grab Montague's left arm. He smashed his right fist into my jaw, but I didn't let go. He let his fist fly at me again. I ducked, seized his right arm, pulled hard, let his momentum carry him over my back, and slammed him onto the floor. I was not gentle. He tried to get up, so I seized his left hand and forced it backward toward his wrist. He groaned in pain and quit resisting.

"Deputy!"

There were a couple of buzzes, and two deputies came running down the corridor. One of them handcuffed Montague's wrist to his ankle. I let go of his hand, and he collapsed onto the floor. Partly carrying and partly dragging him, the deputies took Montague to his cell. "Whose side are you on, anyway?" he shrieked at me.

"The law's side," I replied.

I went over to Rick. He was clutching his left eye. "Rick, you OK?"

"My eye! He got my eye!"

The door buzzed again. Another officer and two men came in. "Hey, what happened?"

"Montague tried to escape," I explained. "He clawed Rick in the eye. I think he's hurt."

"You OK, Rick? Can you walk?" Two men helped him to his feet and led him out.

I leaned against the wall. I was still breathing heavily.

"Are you all right?" one of the deputies asked. I nodded but rubbed my jaw with my hand. It was sore, but it still worked. I had never been slugged in the face before. I wanted to savor the feeling so I could write about it in my journal. All in all, I felt proud of myself.

"Through the window, I saw him sock you," the other deputy said. "I tried to come right in, but there was nobody to buzz me through. But it looks like you didn't need any help. What was that—karate?"

I shook my head. "Judo. Learned it when I was in the Marines in Okinawa."

"Sheesh, you sure threw him around," the deputy said in admiration.

I smiled a little. I felt macho.

My breathing was back to normal now. "Is that usual procedure, to handcuff a wrist to an ankle?" I asked.

The deputy looked worried. "Why, is it illegal?"

"No, I've just never seen it before. Can I talk to my client now?"

"Maybe we'd better let him calm down for a little while," the deputy suggested.

"Can I talk to him from outside his cell?" I asked.

The deputy nodded and led me to Montague's cell. Montague was sitting on his bed, rubbing his hurt wrist.

"Montague, if you ever get out of here, it'll be the law that sets you free."

Montague let loose at me with a torrent of verbal abuse. I didn't respond. He glared at me with impotent fury in his eyes. "Get out of here," he said at last. "You're fired."

I waited until I was in the privacy of my car before I let a wide grin spread over my face. It was worth a sore jaw to hear words like that.

Chapter Nine

The weather the next morning matched my spirits. It was a bright, cloudless day, with a warmth that would lead a person unfamiliar with the vagaries of Utah weather to think that winter was over. But it was only the first Tuesday in March, so we would probably get a few more storms before spring arrived.

I decided that I'd better get down to the humdrum job of tying up all the loose ends on the Montague case so I could turn it over to my replacement. Judge Hastings was going to be ticked, but Montague had fired me for fulfilling my legal duties, and he had that right. I was going to file my motion to be released from the case.

One discrepancy had showed up in my records. Adney Cannest and his wife had both said that the arrest they had witnessed had taken place at ten o'clock. The police records differed slightly. According to the police, the murder victims were discovered by Karen Shears at about 10:10. The all-points bulletin went out at 10:15. Officer Frost reported that he spotted the suspect's Mustang almost immediately thereafter, at 10:17. He then pulled over and arrested the suspects in front of Adney Cannest's yard.

Adney and Elaine's statements that the arrest took place at ten was only a minor discrepancy, probably due to an approximation of the time. But I had to check it out; until released, I was still Montague's attorney and had the duty to follow up on all leads.

Sister Cannest answered the phone.

"Sister Cannest? This is John Lindsey."

"Oh, hello, Bishop."

"Remember when I last talked to you about the arrest that took place in front of your house? You told me that the officer pulled my client over at ten o'clock."

"That's right."

"How did you know that it was ten o'clock? Did you remember looking at a clock, or what?"

"No, but the movie that was on TV that night was just over, and the ten o'clock news was just starting."

"Are you sure that it was just at the start of the news?"

"Well, pretty sure. I remember because, well, you know how it is at the start of the Channel Five news. There's a whole bunch of colored lights in the sky, meteors or comets or something, and those lights come together to make the five. Well, Karen said just as the lights came together, 'Those sure are pretty lights.' Right then we saw the red-and-blue cop lights flash on outside, and Adney said 'There're some not-so-pretty lights,' and we all laughed. We went out to see what was going on. The officer had pulled over that car, and he was just getting out of his own car."

"Did you hear what the officer was saying?"

"No, like I told you before, I stayed up on the porch, so I couldn't hear very well. But it seemed that he was talking really nice, but in a sarcastic kind of way, if you know what I mean. I told you all that before."

"Yes, I know. I'm sorry to bother you again. You didn't tell me about the lights on the TV last time."

"I guess it didn't occur to me. And you didn't ask."

"No, I didn't," I said. "Did Adney stay on the porch with you?"

"For a little while, I guess, then he started edging closer. Maybe he heard better what was going on."

"Did Karen go outside with you?"

"Yes, she and Bobby went right up to where they were talking. They probably heard everything."

"Last time, you didn't tell me they were there."

"You didn't ask."

"When the officer talked to them, how did he act?"

"Well, like I said, at first he was talking nice, but in a sarcastic way."

"If you couldn't hear what he was saying, what did he do that made you think he was being sarcastic?"

"Well, I could hear a little. And it was his tone of voice, real nicey-nice, so you knew he didn't mean a word."

"OK, what happened then?"

"Well, they talked for a while—"

"A long while or a little while?"

"Well, several minutes."

"Five minutes, ten minutes?"

"Five or six minutes, maybe longer."

"Any idea about what they were saying?"

"No."

"Then what happened?"

"Well, it looked like the guy in the car kind of sassed the officer a little, and the cop ordered him out of the car."

"Did you hear him sassing?"

"Well, I didn't hear exactly what was said, but you have kids—you know the tone of voice when someone's sassing you. I did hear the officer order him out of the car. They argued about that for a little while, and then the officer put his hand on his gun, and they got out."

"He drew his gun?"

"No, just put his hand on it. Then he told them, 'Spread 'em'—I heard him say that. He had them spread their arms and legs and lean up against the car. Then he patted the outside of their clothes and reached into their pockets. He pulled things out, and suddenly he drew his gun and yelled at them to lie face down on the snow. He stood there all fiercelike, waving his pistol at them, and he told Adney to call Chief Reitzen on the phone. It looked like the officer was just showing off. I mean, he was being really dramatic. Adney called Brother Reitzen, and a little while later Brother Reitzen and Bishop Alvirez showed up, handcuffed the guys, and put them in the car. So it turned out to be the real thing after all."

"About how much time would you say elapsed between the time your husband made the joke and the time Chief Reitzen arrived?"

"I dunno, fifteen, maybe twenty minutes."

"Can I talk to Adney?"

"He's not here. I don't know when he'll be back."

"Are Karen and Bobby in school?"

"Uh-huh."

"Do you know when their lunch time is?"

"No, but you could call the schools and find out."

I thanked Sister Cannest and hung up. An ugly suspicion was growing in my mind. I dialed information and got a phone number, then dialed again.

"KSL Television. May I help you?" a pleasant female voice said.

"Yes, I'm John Lindsey, an attorney in Sanpete county. I'm calling long distance. I don't know who I should talk to, but I need some information. I need to know your television schedule for last Christmas night, the exact time the ten o'clock news came on. Who would I talk to?"

"That would be our program manager. I'll ring her for you."

I heard another ring.

"Tamara Johnson. May I help you?"

"Are you the program manager?"

"Yes."

"I need to know exactly when your ten o'clock news started last Christmas night. I'm an attorney, and the time might be important to my case."

"Are you suing us?" she asked.

"No, I'm handling a criminal case in Sanpete County. I just need to know if there was any special programming or a football game or something that made the ten o'clock news late."

"I don't remember any. Let me check."

A moment later, she picked up the phone.

"Sir? *Rio Lobo* ended at 9:56, and the *Eyewitness News* started at exactly ten, according to our records."

"Ma'am, you know at the start of the news, how all those colored lights come together to form your logo? Is that shown only at the start of the news?"

"That's right."

"Is there any chance that someone made a mistake and put it in at, say, the middle?"

"No, that didn't happen."

"Could you Xerox a copy of your log or whatever it is that you got your information from? I'll be glad to pay for it."

"That's OK, sir. I'll be glad to send it to you, if you'll give me your name and address."

I gave it to her, and hung up. I called the high school and the junior high next and found out Karen and Bobby's lunchtimes. Then I sat back and waited. I tried not to think about what I was going to find out.

At eleven, I went over to Manti High and talked to Karen. Then I talked to Bobby at the junior high.

I drove home slowly, and parked the car in my driveway. I took my suit coat into the house, hung it up, and went back outside. I walked down our street for a quarter of a mile to where the asphalt ended and the hill began. I climbed the hill for about ten minutes until I came to a place that leveled off for some twenty yards before sloping steeply up again. I sat down on a big rock to catch my breath.

I was at what my kids term the "Family Knoll." Geologically and legally, the term was incorrect. The flat spot was not a knoll, and it was owned by the United States Government. But when we had first moved into Ammon, we found the little spot to be a convenient place for picnics, family home evening programs, and assorted activities. The kids slept there a lot. We had planted a bunch of trees there and carried water to them for the first few summers until the trees got established. The spot was about four hundred feet above the valley floor and gave an unrestricted view of Ammon, Ephraim, and Manti.

I quietly sat in the warm sunshine. Cars that appeared as small as insects crawled up and down the highway. The green lawns of the towns contrasted sharply with the brown and yellow of farmlands in between. In the distance, the temple gleamed in the bright sunlight.

For over two hours I struggled.

Finally I came down from the hill, got in my car, and drove to the courthouse.

In his private office, I found Kurt Vanderhoft with his feet on his desk.

"Kurt, I think you've got some problems."

"I've got lots of problems, John. What's on your mind?"

"Russell Montague and Bryan Sanchez were pulled over at exactly ten P.M. The APB went out at ten-fifteen."

"So?" he said with polite indifference.

I didn't say anything.

"So what?"

I still didn't say anything.

I watched his face in metamorphosis. The look of unconcern melted into a look of doubt. He took his feet off his desk, and they hit the floor heavily.

Kurt leaned forward. "What did the arrest report say? Why was he arrested?"

"Murder."

"Didn't it say anything about a traffic violation, or anything?"

"No."

"How do you know they were pulled over at ten?"

"I have at least three witnesses. Adney Cannest's wife and two oldest kids. Probably Adney too. The kids say that the arresting officer pulled them over and harassed them about their hair. Ordered them out of the car when they sassed back. Frisked them. Conducted an illegal search and seizure. That's when he found the wallet."

Kurt slammed his desk top with his fist. "Another redneck cop!" he exploded. After a moment he put his face into his hands.

He finally raised his head. "Who was the arresting officer? Frost, wasn't it?"

"Yes."

Kurt rubbed his chin. He was silent for a while. Then he gave me a quizzical glance. "John, does anyone else know about this?" he asked in a quiet, conspiratorial tone.

"Why?"

Kurt's face became earnest, almost pleading. "We can't let these guys get away like this." He looked at me meaningfully, imploringly.

With a shock, I realized what Kurt was asking. Kurt had always been one hundred percent straight, even though his motives were sometimes political.

"If those guys go free, you don't stand a chance of getting elected next fall," he said intently.

It also occurred to me that it wouldn't do his chances any good either. "Kurt, I can't believe what you're suggesting. Several weeks ago, when this was an open-and-shut case, you wanted me to fight like all get out. But now that you'll have to work a little to get a conviction, you're asking me to violate my oath to obey the law?" It surprised me, because even without the wallet and money, he still would get a conviction. A witness had seen Montague's car, and most important, the recovering victim was an eyewitness to all the events.

"I'm going to talk to Chief Reitzen," I said. "You want to come along?"

Kurt stood up and grabbed my shoulder.

"John."

I shook his hand off. "You coming?"

I walked out of his office. He didn't follow me.

I found Chief Reitzen at the police station. He said that Frost was on traffic control on the north end of town. But he wasn't. The police car was parked outside Betty's Home Cooking. We went inside. Frost was sitting at a table, talking and laughing with a group of the local yokels.

"Randy," Chief Reitzen said sternly. Frost looked up, and the smile faded from his face.

"Oh, hi, Chief. I just dropped in for a quick cup of coffee. Got to stay alert out there, you know."

"You took a whole Thermos-full with you. Come on. We need to talk to you."

We went next door to my office. I'm not nearly as brutally effective an interrogator as Kurt is, but by the time the questioning was through, there were no doubts in our minds. Frost had pulled my client over not because he had broken any law, but because he was a long-haired hippie freak.

Frost had noticed them when they stopped at the Iceburger to eat, and he had waited until they drove away to pull them over. But Frost felt he had honorable motives for doing so. In the small Wyoming town Frost had come from, the police chief had told him the secret to having a good, respectable town. He said that most crimes were committed by drifters, hippies, and other no-accounts. If the police kept their eyes open and roughed up all such people as soon as they entered town, the word would soon get around and no troublemakers would dare pass through, thus making life pleasant for the decent folks.

"Randy, after John told me about you harassing his kid, I thought I'd made it clear to you to knock it off," Chief Reitzen remarked.

"You just talked about local kids. You didn't say anything about out-of-towners. These guys had Arizona license plates."

Chief Reitzen shook his head in disgust.

"I was just doing what I figured was best for the town," Frost said in an injured tone.

"OK. Let's go get your car, then I'll take you home."

"I've still got two hours left on my shift," Frost said.

"Don't worry about that," Chief Reitzen growled. "You're fired."

After the police left, I made a long-distance phone call to Los Angeles. Bryan Sanchez's family had hired a criminal attorney in L.A. to handle their son's case, and Bryan had let Brent Crenshaw go. They'd made a mistake in hiring an attorney who was so far away that he couldn't really devote much time to Bryan's defense, not to mention the bucks they lost by hiring private counsel when Bryan could have been represented for free. But I guess they just didn't trust us hicks. In fact, Ralph Hersh, the new attorney, could do no more for Bryan than Brent could do. But it wasn't my money, so I didn't complain.

Hersh's secretary said that he wasn't in. I left a message for him to call me. Then I took off for Richfield.

"How's Rick doing?" I asked the jailor inside the glass booth who buzzed me in.

"Oh, hi, Mr. Lindsey. Thanks for helping that time. Rick's got some scratches on one of his eyes. Didn't touch his cornea, though, so he'll be OK. But he's still in some pain."

Another jailor went to get Montague. He came back shortly. "He doesn't want to speak to you."

"Tell him I have important news. He'll want to hear it."

A moment later, Montague was led into the small room where I was waiting. He had shackles on his legs, and his hands were handcuffed behind him.

"Do they keep you like this all the time?"

He shook his head. "What's up? The jailor said it was really important."

"Tell me exactly what happened the night you were arrested. What did you say to the officer who pulled you over, and what did he say to you?"

"That's all you want to talk about? I thought you had something important. Besides, I've told you what happened."

"Not in much detail. Tell me about that night. It's important."

"Is it good news, or bad news?"

"For you, good news. Tell me what happened that night."

"Well, the flashing lights came on, and I thought, 'We've

had it.' So I pulled over, and this fat pig comes to my window and I roll it down. Then this pig says something like, 'Well, it looks like they've let the animals out of the zoo.' I asked him what he wanted because maybe he didn't know about the shooting yet. I was really polite, thought I'd see if I could talk my way out of it. He says stuff like 'Looks like we have a couple of shaggy beasts here,' and then he talks about getting some of the boys together for a sheep-shearing party. I decided that he didn't have anything on us, he just didn't like our hair. So I said something like, 'Beat it, pig, you got nothing on us,' and he got mad. He quit grinning and orders me and Sanchez out of the car. I told him to drop dead. Then he really yells, puts his hand on his gun, and tells me and Sanchez to get out. So we got out. Then he said, 'Spread 'em,' so we did. Then he frisked us. When he pulled the wallet out and saw that it was sticky with blood, he drew his gun. He made us lie down on the snow with our hands behind our heads. Then he yelled to some people to call some more cops. And he stood over us for a while, pointing the gun at us and calling us names, until another cop car came." He stopped for a second. "Hey, he never read us our rights!" he said with a grin.

"Officer Alvirez said that he read them to you himself."

"Yeah, the second cop did, but does that count? The arresting cop never read them to us!"

"You're barking up the wrong tree, Russell." I paused for a minute to collect my thoughts.

"Our forefathers were continually harassed by a repressive government that would invade their homes at all hours, trying to find evidence of crimes that may have been committed or merely to harass them and make their lives miserable," I said in a flat, schoolteacher's voice. I needed to explain this to myself as well as to him.

"As a result, when our forefathers started their own country, they tacked onto their new Constitution a provision that says, 'The right of the people to be secure in their persons, houses, and effects against unreasonable searches and seizures shall not be violated, and no warrants shall be issued, but upon probable cause . . . ,'" I quoted imperfectly. "By interpretation, *probable cause* means that the state must have reason to believe that you have committed a crime before they can search you or your effects or detain or arrest you. If the police search you without probable cause, then the United States Supreme Court says that whatever they seize cannot be used against you in court. The officer who pulled you over did not have reason to believe you had committed a crime when he pulled you over. He pulled you over because of your hair. So, the prosecution can't use the wallet or the money against you."

A smile spread over his face. "You mean what they have against me is illegal? They can't use it against me? I can get out of here?" He almost shrieked his last words.

"Hold it—not that far. You're not out of here. The wallet and money can't be used against you, but there is still the little matter of the surviving victim. And the woman who saw your car parked outside the cleaners."

"You mean they've still got me?" His face fell.

"Your victim has supposedly come out of her coma. It remains to be seen what she remembers about that night. But this might give you some plea-bargaining leverage. The odds are still against you, but maybe the prosecutor will be willing to talk to you now."

"I should have blown that retard's brains away!" he said viciously. He felt no remorse, only regret that he had done such a sloppy job that the victim recovered.

"You think I have any chance in court now for an acquittal?" he inquired.

I shook my head. "Not much of one. I think that your best hope might be negotiating with Kurt for life imprisonment instead of the death penalty."

He sat quietly for a moment. "No, Bishop. I'm going ahead with the trial. As long as I have any ghost of a chance, I'll trust my luck. An acquittal or death. Life in prison won't do me any good. But if I get out, I have a long, exciting life ahead of me. All or nothing!"

"Suits me just fine," I replied. "I'd just as soon see you get the death penalty than have to support you in prison for the rest of your life. I'll let your new defense counselor worry about it. I've got the motion for a new attorney all ready to turn in."

He looked at me intently, and a malicious smile slowly spread over his face. "No, Bishop, I'm not going to let you off so easy. I think I'll keep you. Before, I was a dead man. But now, thanks to you, there's an outside chance that I'll be on the streets again. And if I lose, I'll drag you down with me." He laughed. "Bishop, I'm going to enjoy watching you squirm."

"Dream on, Montague," I replied dryly. "They're going to blow you away."

At my office later that afternoon, Ralph Hersh returned my call. As I expected, he'd been planning a plea bargain for San-chez in return for his testimony against Montague. I told him about the illegal search-and-seizure evidence I'd uncovered.

"You think I ought to ride this out with my client in the hope of an acquittal instead of a plea bargain?" he asked.

"That's your decision. My client is going for an acquittal."

"Well, at least I can wait and see how things turn out."

"You do what you think is best for your client," I replied, but I hoped that Sanchez would help put Montague away for good.

At eleven o'clock that night the phone rang just as I was get-ting into bed. I reached over and grabbed the receiver.

"Hello?"

"John, this is Kurt. I just heard something, and if I can't sleep tonight, I'm not going to let you sleep either."

"What are you talking about?"

"Have you heard that Wendy Wainsgaard has come out of her coma?"

"Yeah, your secretary mentioned it. It's true then?"

"Yeah, she's awake. But some information hasn't been re-leased yet."

"What's that?"

"The bullet went through the sight portion of her brain. I have no eyewitness. She's blind."

Chapter Ten

For the next several weeks, I diligently fulfilled all of my paternal, religious, and legal duties. By submerging myself in my work, I hoped to forget the horror of Kurt's revelation. But it loomed on the edge of my consciousness like a thundercloud approaching a picnic. The calm I displayed on the surface did not reflect the tumult within, and my feelings had started to manifest themselves tangibly by some brief but sharp stomach pains. I had always considered myself to be too well adjusted to have problems like that. I tried to ignore them.

I knew that for justice to prevail, Wendy Wainsgaard would have to be able to describe her assailants with meticulous accuracy. A blind witness could not simply point to the defendants and say, "They did it." In the ensuing weeks, I attempted to get a meeting with Wendy Wainsgaard to determine just how effective a witness she would be. Ralph Hersh made daily calls nagging me to interview her. He obviously wanted to know what kind of bargaining power he would have with Kurt. I resented Hersh's harassment. He had only been up here once to see his client, apparently feeling that he could rely on me to handle things without his presence. His only expected duty seemed to be showing up for his check when everything was over.

I was not being derelict in my efforts to contact Wendy. Kurt had said that he wanted to be present when I talked to her, and he knew where she was. I didn't. But he kept postponing my appointments to see Wendy, until I began to wonder if he were deliberately stalling.

I broke my pencil in frustration late one afternoon in early April as I sat in my office fighting with my tax forms and records. While in my disgruntled mood, Mrs. Henderson buzzed on the intercom and told me that Ralph Hersh was on the line again.

"John Lindsey here," I said.

"John, this is Ralph Hersh. Have you talked to the Wainsgaard girl yet?"

"Not yet. I talked to Kurt, and he said that he'd try to arrange something by the end of the week."

"Isn't that what he said last week? Listen, John, that trial is only about a month away. We have to know what kind of evidence the prosecutor will be able to produce, and the girl is the key. So get on it."

"I will."

"I mean right now."

"Look, Ralph, if you don't like what I'm doing or the way I'm doing it, why don't you just hop on a jet, head up here, and do it yourself? Get off my back!" I slammed the receiver down. The pain in my gut became noticeable. As I sat there, I began to regret my rudeness. It wasn't like me. But I didn't care to be ordered around by Hersh like I was one of his flunkies.

However, Hersh had a point. I picked up the phone and dialed a number.

"Hello?"

"Kurt, this is John. I'm going to talk to Wendy Wainsgaard tomorrow. You want to go with me?"

He cleared his throat. "Can't make it tomorrow, John. But how about if I plan something for us by the end of the week?"

"No good, Kurt. You said that last week. You have no right to keep her from me if she's willing to talk to me. Where is she staying?"

"I'm . . . not sure. Maybe she's still with her aunt in Payson. But I understand that she was going to start at that training center for the blind, so maybe she's there."

"What's her aunt's name? I'll give her a call right now."

"I forget. I've got it written somewhere at the office, I think. Why don't you call me tomorrow night, or the next day?"

"They've got a cousin in Ephraim. I'll call her right now and find out the aunt's name. I'm going tomorrow—the trial is in one month, and we need to know where my client stands. If you want to come with me tomorrow, you're welcome. If you're busy, too bad. But I'm going."

There was silence for a moment. "OK. I'll call you in the morning, see what I can arrange."

"First thing?"

"First thing." He hung up without saying good-bye.

I hung up the phone too. I walked to the window and stared out, tensing myself against the pain that was again gnawing at my vitals.

Chapter Eleven

Kurt Vanderhoft called before eight o'clock the next morning, just as he had promised. He reported that he would pick me up about ten and take me to see Wendy in Payson. I replied that I had a doctor's appointment in Provo, so I'd prefer to drive myself. He gave me her aunt's address and told me to meet him there about eleven o'clock.

After Kurt called, I took off for Provo. I pulled into the parking lot at the Timpanogos Medical Center, then walked into one of the offices and told the receptionist that I wished to see Dr. Rogers. She replied that she didn't see my name on the appointment book. I explained that I didn't need an appointment and asked her to tell Dr. Rogers that John Lindsey was there to see him.

Some two decades earlier, Warren Rogers and I had been rivals for Carol Robinson's affections. I won hands down. That surprised me, because I thought Warren was a better man than I. He was a premed student at the Y and came from a well-to-do family. He took first in state in cross-country and the mile run and received a track scholarship from BYU. On his mission, he was an assistant to the mission president. He had a nice personality and was a true spiritual giant. Yet, when I came home from my mission and met Carol at the Y, she deserted Warren immediately. I knew a good thing when I saw it, and we quickly got engaged. I was secretly astounded though, that a girl with her qualities would leave a guy like Warren for a guy like me. It really shattered my trust in her judgment. Like most women, as soon as Carol knew she had me, she immediately tried to change me. She informed me that she would not marry a career military officer. I had my heart set on a career in the Marines and believed that it was none of her business how I made my living as long as I was honorably employed and kept the rent paid. The deadlock continued with neither of us willing to change. Finally, she broke off the engagement. Carol and I were both miserable, but neither of us would give in.

Warren came over to my place one night and told me that he loved Carol and would make a better husband for her than I would. I resented his comments because I secretly felt he was right. But then he went on to say that he was afraid that she'd spend the rest of her life moping for me unless she and I got married. Warren acted as mediator in the negotiations of a compromise between Carol and me. But he refused to come to our wedding, explaining that he wasn't a glutton for punishment.

Warren won my respect at the Y and my friendship in Vietnam. He was a navy doctor at the hospital to which I was taken when I was shot and critically wounded. I handled his legal problems now, and he took care of my medical problems. He told me that I never needed an appointment, though that didn't mean he could immediately see me. I cooled my heels in the waiting room for a while until a nurse called me in. I waited some more in a colorful room decorated with cutouts of Sleepy, Grumpy, Happy, and Dopey.

After a few geological ages, Doctor Rogers came in with a smile. "Hello, John, did you get my check?"

"Yeah, I did. You ding-dong, I meant that bill as a joke."

"Well, it served me right," he said grinning.

I had last seen Warren at the Republican State Convention. While he and I were shooting the breeze, a woman he knew came up to him and told him about some aches and pains she was having. He gave her an on-the-spot examination and prescribed a treatment. After she left, Warren complained that no matter where he was, people kept hitting him for free medical advice. He then asked me if he had the legal right to send that woman a bill for services rendered. I told him that he did. He was pleased and went home and billed the woman. The next day, he received my bill.

"Well, what's your problem?" he asked.

I described my symptoms to him. He looked at me thoughtfully.

"Are you still a bishop, John?"

"Yes. Over five-and-a-half years now."

"You enjoy being bishop?"

"It has its positive and its negative points. Occasionally I look forward to being released, to when my time will become my own again. But most of the time, I realize that next to my marriage, it's the greatest experience of my life. But it can be trying."

"Has it been particularly trying recently?"

"We have some money problems, but on the other hand, attendance at meetings and the temple is way up. We've had our ups and downs, but each time I notice that the ups are a little higher and the lows aren't quite so low. All in all, I have to admit that I enjoy it."

"You say you've been bishop for more than five years? In our stake, they generally release a bishop after five years. Is it different in your stake?"

"No, in our stake, five years is generally the limit," I admitted. "But the stake president asked me to continue."

"Maybe you'd better ask to be released."

"Why?"

He sighed. "John, I'm sure you must have suspected that you have a peptic ulcer. That's what it sounds like to me. We'll try to make sure before you leave. I know a bishop who had to be released after a year and a half because of the ulcers he developed. Looks like yours took a little longer. It's stressful work, and some guys' systems can't handle the conflicts. It's nothing to be ashamed of. But John, you're literally eating yourself up right now. We can treat you, but unless we resolve the conflicts and get rid of the stress, it won't do any good. It doesn't sound to me like your ulcer amounts to much yet. We can probably control it with a proper diet, but only if you can get rid of the problems that caused the ulcers in the first place. Ask the stake president to release you. Tell him it's doctor's orders."

"Warren, I'm not going to ask to be released."

"John, don't be stupid. This isn't Vietnam—you don't have to prove how tough you are."

"It's not my Church job that's tearing me apart. I'm handling a criminal defense case that's making me question the values they taught me in law school."

"Oh? Tell me about it."

"I can't, Warren. There's a gag order in effect."

"Can you get out of the case for health reasons?"

I shook my head. "Ulcers are an occupational hazard for defense attorneys. A lot of them hit the booze hard too. I'll settle for an ulcer."

"When will it all be over?"

"In another month."

He shrugged. "Well, I'll do what I can for you. The nurse'll give you a chart with a diet on it. I hope you know someone who owns a dairy."

At eleven o'clock I searched the back streets of Payson for an address. I found Kurt's Volvo parked outside a well-kept older home. As I pulled into the driveway, Kurt stepped outside onto the porch.

Forty-five minutes later, he and I walked out of the house together. I held my peace until we reached my car.

"Kurt," I said in a low voice, "if you put that girl on the stand, I'll cut her to pieces."

"What're you talking about? She's a competent witness."

"She's a parrot. She'll repeat anything you tell her to say. She'd testify that John Wilkes Booth shot her if you told her to."

"That's not fair, John. She has a recollection of the events of that night."

"You've coached her on everything she says, and she still doesn't say it well. You can't coach her during cross-ex, Kurt. When you kept your mouth shut in there, I got her to change her story twice. You might be able to lead her by the nose when she gives her story, but when I get her I'll butcher her. How's a blind girl going to identify her assailants, huh?"

"She can describe what they looked like, and she can identify their voices," Kurt replied.

"You're going to try to base a conviction on that? You're going for the death penalty based on voice identification by a mentally deficient woman? Haven't you ever heard the term 'guilty beyond a reasonable doubt'? How can you prove beyond a reasonable doubt that my client is guilty, based on such flimsy evidence? There's no way in the world you can do that."

"Why don't we let the jury decide that?" Kurt remarked.

"Why?" I retorted. "Because the ethics of a prosecutor are supposed to require you to drop a prosecution when you know you don't have enough evidence to support a conviction. Even if the jury convicts through passion or prejudice, you know the judge will arrest judgment, and if she doesn't, the Supreme Court will overturn it."

"Listen, John, I'm the county attorney. This is *my* decision, and I'm going to prosecute this case!"

"Kurt, you don't even have a case, and you're too much of a politicking coward to admit it!"

Kurt turned a deep red. I turned around and got into my car. I backed out and punched the accelerator. The squealing protest from my tires matched what I felt inside.

I slowed down a moment later when I passed a policeman who had pulled over another speedster. It was a long drive home. I wanted to get up and pace in the front seat while I wrestled with my thoughts.

I parked my car outside my office. I said a brusque hello to Mrs. Henderson and shut the door behind me as I went into my private office. I tried to do some work but couldn't concentrate. I walked out of the office, went to Betty's next door, and bought an overpriced carton of milk. I brought it back to my office, shut the door again, and quickly guzzled the milk. I crushed the carton and threw it into the wastebasket, then put my head on my desk and buried my face in my arms. For a long time I just sat.

I finally stood up and got my portable typewriter from the closet. I couldn't find any typing paper, so I went out and asked Mrs. Henderson for a few sheets.

"Do you want me to do some typing for you?" she asked.

I shook my head. "This is personal." She gave me a few sheets.

"Mrs. Sylvan from the *Ammon Advocate* called and wanted to talk to you about the Wainsgaard case," she said.

"Well, I don't want to talk to the press about this case."

"She didn't want to know about the case so much; she wanted background information on you, since you're handling the case. I gave her some and told her to call Carol about the stuff I couldn't answer. Is that OK?"

"Sure."

"You're going to get famous from this case," she observed.

"It's not the kind of thing I want to be famous for."

"Did you read the *Gunnison Valley News?* They had an article about this case. Did you know that this is the first murder in the county since the Depression?"

"So I've heard."

"Sister Rupert says that they had an article about our case in the *Manti Messenger* too, but I haven't seen it yet. Do you think we'll get television crews down here?"

"Probably."

She looked concerned for a moment. "Do you think I ought to get a new hairdo?"

I wanted to shout that I didn't care about her hair, but instead I turned around and went back into my office.

I sat at my desk and typed for a few minutes. I looked at what I had written, tore it up, and started over. After three tries, I had what I wanted. I got up and told Mrs. Henderson that I'd be back in about half an hour. I drove home and asked Carol if she knew where my gloves were. She said they were right where they were supposed to be. I looked in the coat closet and sure enough, there they were. But after putting them on, I decided they were too thick for my current needs, so I put them back into the closet and drove to the 7-Eleven. I picked out a pair of cheap, thin gloves and handed the money to the checker. I hoped that I didn't look as guilty as I felt.

"Going to do some gardening, Bishop?" she asked.

"I'll do some next Saturday," I replied.

She handed me the change and my receipt, and I left. I briefly wondered if the gloves were tax deductible because they were job related. But considering the use I intended for them I decided not to claim them. I threw the receipt away as I left the store.

I drove a few miles past Manti to the old shack where the gun was hidden, keeping a close eye on the odometer as I went. Then I made a U-turn and drove to Ephraim. I stopped at Snow College and went into the library to the typing room. A student was inside, so I didn't go in but instead went to the bookstore and bought a package of typing paper and some envelopes. When I went back to the typing room, the student was still there. I sat down in a chair that faced the room and picked up a book, pretending to read about amoebas and paramecia as I watched the door. Finally the girl left. Pretending to be casual, I strolled to the typing room. Once inside, I quickly shut the door, put on the gloves, tore open the package of envelopes, and typed the address of the state crime lab in Richfield on an envelope. I tore open the package of typing paper, put a sheet in the typewriter, and quickly typed one line: "Re. Wainsgaard murder—have you thoroughly searched abandoned house 2.7 miles south of Manti for murder weapon?"

I put the letter in the envelope. I was about to lick the flap on the envelope but suddenly wondered if saliva were traceable, so I folded the flap inside. I took the glove off my left hand and shoved my gloved right hand and the envelope into my pants pocket. I was startled when the door opened.

"Oh, hi, Mr. Lindsey. Doing a little typing?"

It was Marcy Cavendish. Brenda had been her campaign manager in high school when Marcy had successfully run for student-body president.

"Hi, Marcy. Yeah, just finished."

"How's Brenda doing at the Y? Is she engaged yet?"

We talked briefly about Brenda, then I excused myself, promising Marcy that I'd tell Brenda hi for her.

I walked over to the post office and bought a book of stamps. I went outside, and when I was sure no one was looking, I stuck the corner of my handkerchief into the gutter to moisten it, then touched the back of the stamp with it. I firmly affixed the stamp onto the envelope. I got in my car and drove south past Ammon, Manti, and Sterling. In Gunnison I parked on the roadside by a big blue-and-red mailbox.

I leaned forward and rested my head on the steering wheel. I heard a car pull up behind me and heard its door slam. I listened to the driver's footsteps on the gravel and heard the mailbox chute clang shut. The footsteps returned, hesitated, and suddenly there was a slight tapping on my window. I looked up. A young mother carrying her baby was looking at me with concern.

"Are you OK, sir?"

"What?"

"Are you all right?"

I nodded.

"Are you sure?"

I nodded again. "Yeah."

She looked at me doubtfully, then walked back to her car, got in, and drove away.

I stared at the mailbox. After a while, I opened the car door, got out, and sluggishly walked over to the mailbox. I slowly pulled the handle of the chute down, held it open for a moment, then pulled the letter from my pocket. I set the letter precariously on the edge of the chute and gazed at it for several minutes.

Finally, I picked the letter back up, put it into my pocket, and let go of the chute handle. It clanged shut. I walked back to my car, hesitated, and pulled the letter out. After a moment's indecision, I tore it into tiny pieces. I walked across the street and threw some of the pieces into a trashcan that urged me to help keep Gunnison beautiful. I drove back north, stopping in Sterling and Manti to drop off a few more of the pieces into trashcans. I deposited the last of the pieces in a trashcan outside of Betty's Home Cooking. I walked into my law office, mumbled a greeting to Mrs. Henderson, went back into my private office, and shut the door. I sat down at my desk and once more buried my face in my arms.

Chapter Twelve

The *Gunnison Valley News* was only the first paper that week to contain an article about the upcoming murder trial. By the end of the week, the *Mount Pleasant Pyramid, Ephraim Enterprise, Manti Messenger,* and *Ammon Advocate* all had stories about the Wainsgaard and Coombs murders. The *Manti Messenger* included biographies of Mrs. Wainsgaard and Aaron Coombs. The *Ammon Advocate,* desperate for a local angle, included an article about me. The information in the article was accurate, but the picture of me was an ancient one, dating from ten years before when I had first run for the city council. Carol told me that no one would notice because I had a boyish face that made me look ten years younger than I really was. She's a sweet liar.

On Monday morning, I arrived at my office at eight o'clock, as usual. Mrs. Henderson was due in at eight-thirty. Eight-thirty came, but Mrs. Henderson didn't, nor did she call to say she'd be late.

Alice Henderson was in her late fifties. She suffered from multiple sclerosis. I had first met her years before at the local nursing home. She had been hospitalized for over a year and was apparently dying when her husband divorced her. I thought he must be a heck of a creep to divorce a dying wife and remarry a neighborhood widow shortly thereafter. But Mrs. Henderson claimed she had no ill will toward him. She said he felt really guilty about the whole situation. I should hope so. Soon after he dumped Alice, her multiple sclerosis went into partial remission, and she was released from the hospital. All of her children offered to let her live with them, but she turned them down, not wanting to be a burden. Instead, since she had relatives in Ammon, she left her home in Logan and put herself in the nursing home here. Having placed herself on the shelf to rot, she spent her time watching soap operas. We held sacrament meeting at the nursing home every week, which is how I met her. I listened to her story and suggested that she do something with herself, but she was convinced she could no longer be useful.

Shortly thereafter, my cousin, who was my legal secretary, informed me that she was pregnant and would leave in a few months. Mrs. Henderson had once said that she could type seventy words a minute, so I asked her if she wanted the job. She was reluctant at first, doubting her ability to live on her own, but with some government assistance, she got a specially equipped car and an apartment with ramps. She really was an exceptional typist, but unfortunately she was also an inveterate gossip. She spent lots of time on the office phone talking to friends until I finally cracked down and forbade personal phone calls during office hours. So her friends came to the office instead, which I also had to forbid, except at lunchtime. Worst of all, she was somewhat careless in her work, an unpardonable sin in an attorney's office. When Nick Hansen got a default judgment against one of my clients because Mrs. Henderson had neglected to do some scheduling on my calender, I fired her. Since my client hadn't had his day in court, we got the judgment vacated, and no permanent harm was done. But it made the judge angry at me and made me look like a fool to my client. I prized my reputation for thoroughness and efficiency too much to let her ruin it. Mrs. Henderson tearfully removed her things from her desk and left.

Later that day I heard that she was leaving her apartment and moving back to the nursing home. I suspected that it was a ploy to get my sympathy, but it worked. I went over and offered to give her back her job if she straightened up. She agreed, and pretty much kept her agreement. She became an adequate if not exceptional secretary. But she had one strong point that I had never seen in an employee before; she didn't mind running personal errands for her boss. Once she became strong enough to use a walker, she enjoyed going out and doing things for me. I was notoriously bad at remembering birthdays, anniversaries, and other assorted dates that wives put a great deal of value on, but Mrs. Henderson always remembered and had a gift purchased and wrapped. Unlike me, she remembered Carol's sizes and had good taste. I was content to keep her.

When Mrs. Henderson hadn't shown up by a quarter after nine, I phoned her apartment. There was no answer. A few minutes later she parked outside and came in. I could tell from the expression on her face that something was wrong.

"Hello, Alice."

She didn't say anything. Suddenly her lower lip began trembling and she started to cry. She mumbled something, but I couldn't understand her.

"What?" I asked.

With an effort, she made her speech clearer—"I guess I'd better quit." She continued to weep.

"How come?"

She tried to say something but could no longer speak clearly enough. Finally she opened her purse, fumbled around in it, and pulled out an envelope. She handed me the letter inside.

Dear Sister (ha!) Henderson,

How could you stand in front of the Relief Society this morning, acting so pious and holy, when you are helping that traiter boss of yours defend the murderer of a sweet woman like Sister Wainsgaard? I'm surprised that the man who calls himself Bishop isn't kicked out and excommunicated, and run out of town. And since you're helping him, you deserve no better. I hope he makes a lot of blood money defending those murderers, because he's never going to get another cent from the decent people of this valley. You both are going to be singing for your supper pretty soon. Don't you have any conscience? Don't you feel anything for Wendy Wainsgaard left blind and alone, and Sister Coombs and all those kids? How can you sleep at night? And yet you are helping the man who is helping those murderers!

There is a God in heaven, and someday you and your precious boss are going to face Him and have to account for your monsterous crimes.

I only hope you can accept this letter in the spirit of love, as I intended.

The letter was unsigned.

"You're quitting because of this?" I asked.

She nodded.

"Alice, are you going to let a vicious letter like this get to you?"

She didn't say anything, but kept crying.

"Why don't you sit down," I said gently. I tried for several minutes to talk her out of it, but she didn't respond. "Alice," I finally asked, "do you really want to go?"

She nodded.

"Are you going back to the nursing home?"

She shook her head. I waited until her sobs subsided.

"What're you going to do?"

She wouldn't look at me. "I called my daughter Missy this morning. She said she and her husband would be glad to have me."

"Is she the one who lives in Brigham City?"

She nodded.

"Are you going to get another job?"

"I guess so. I'll try," she said.

"If you're sure you want to leave, I'll be glad to recommend you to any prospective employers," I offered.

"Thank you."

"Could you stay on until the end of the week?"

She shook her head. "My daughter's coming with their truck tomorrow to get my things."

"Can you at least stay until the end of the day today?"

She shook her head. "I need to pack. And I have to pay some bills."

"Alice, can't you handle that after quitting time? I need someone here till the end of the day. I can't get someone else at a minute's notice."

She hesitated.

"You owe me that much, Alice."

"OK," she murmured.

I went home at noon, feeling betrayed. I had given Alice a job at a time when no one else would. I had trained her at my own expense, paid her well, and forgiven her shortcomings. Yet she was abandoning me at the first sign of trouble. It was a grim omen.

At home, I found Carol coming out of the garage with a chisel borrowed from my tool box.

"What'cha doing?" I asked.

"Trying to scrape burnt baked beans from a pot," she replied.

"I can borrow a jackhammer," I said, forcing a joke.

In reply, she handed me the pot and chisel. I excavated and blasted as I told Carol of Mrs. Henderson's desertion in the face of the enemy. I hadn't been able to find any replacements in spite of a flurry of phone calls. Apparently, no one wanted to work for me.

"Why don't you give Lisa a call?" Carol suggested.

My wife amazes me.

Annalisa Johansen, called "Annie" by her folks and "Lisa" by everyone else, is the granddaughter of one of my father's older sisters. She was my legal secretary before Mrs. Henderson. She is also the only girl besides Carol that I have been deeply in love with, years ago, when I was in my early twenties.

After returning from my mission, I went to Richfield and stayed for a while to visit. Among the many relatives who welcomed me home was my cousin Lisa. She was so lovely she melted my heart. She and my sister Shayla were the most beautiful women I knew. But unlike Shayla, Lisa was very sweet. She had everything I ever thought I wanted in a wife. She responded to my interest, and I quickly fell in love. But there were complications. The least serious one was my worry that people would think I was robbing the cradle. It was true—I was twenty-two and she was a high school senior—but there existed a far more serious problem.

My great-grandfather had three wives. His third wife was my great-grandmother Annie. Annie was a full-blooded Paiute Indian. By the standards of either the Indians or the whites, she was incredibly ugly. I know that my great-grandfather earned his place in heaven when he married her. But just as in mathematics, where a negative times a negative equals a positive, when a plain-faced Mormon pioneer started multiplying with an ugly squaw, they produced children of extraordinary beauty.

The strain of loveliness that they bequeathed to their descendants has still not faded away, but it has proved both a blessing and a curse. It was a blessing in that physically attractive people tend to be able to choose their own mates. It was a curse in that attractive people tend to marry attractive people, and the best-looking people in Richfield were all descendants of Annie Lindsey. As a result, there was a great deal of intermarriage among relatives. After a few generations of these interfamilial marriages, several of the offspring developed *lupus erythematosus,* a degenerative disease that slowly kills many of its victims, mostly women. The cause for it is unknown, and there is no cure. It has occurred in several isolated intermountain communities where families constantly intermarried.

I thought I was being quite discreet in my courting of Lisa, but somebody noticed. Lisa's father approached my mother, told her what a fine young man I was, and told her to tell me to bug off. Mom was very subtle. She never lectured me nor even let on that she knew about Lisa and me. She simply took me to visit two of my distant cousins who couldn't come to family reunions because they were in a nursing home, dying of lupus. She even remarkéd that perhaps it was a blessing in disguise that my father's first wife and infant girl had died, since my father's first marriage was to his cousin.

I was badly shaken by what I saw in the nursing home. I was still very much in love with Lisa. I was willing to wait for her until she was old enough to become my wife without her parents' permission. And for her, I was willing to face the unanimous opposition of the entire Lindsey clan. I was even willing to move to another state that recognized marriage between first cousins once removed. But I was not willing to face the prospect of someday seeing my daughters suffer as my cousins in the nursing home were suffering. So I tried to turn my emotions off. I forced myself to be cold and distant with Lisa the next time I saw her, almost to the point of cruelty. Lisa was bewildered and hurt by the change in me, but it was the only way I could cope emotionally with what I felt I had to do. I hoped that her meddling father would explain the situation to her, because I couldn't. I especially hoped that she would realize that I didn't senselessly jilt her.

I enrolled at BYU, where I was shortly to meet and fall in love with Carol. Lisa got married several years later to a college athletic star.

Carol was blessed with an exceptionally nosy disposition and eventually found out the story about Lisa and me. To my surprise, Carol felt no jealous reaction towards Lisa. In fact, Carol and Lisa became very close friends, and Carol would drive down to Richfield every month or so and have lunch with her.

The two were superficially quite dissimilar: Carol was tall, with light brown hair and fair eyes, while Lisa was a petite, dark-haired beauty. But they both had a hard core of incredible goodness. I felt that Carol was almost incapable of making significant mistakes. But Lisa had a touch of human frailty and had made at least one serious mistake—her choice of a marriage partner.

When I set up my practice in Ammon, I was without a legal secretary. Carol found out that Lisa had just lost her job. Without discussing it with me, Carol asked Lisa if she wanted to work for me. Though Richfield is forty-seven miles from Ammon, in those days gas was cheap and the speed limit was higher, so commuting every day was no big deal. Lisa agreed to come. I was disturbed when I found out about the deal Carol and Lisa had arranged. I wasn't sure if I could work comfortably with Lisa. I didn't know whether she understood why I had felt compelled to leave her, and I still felt guilty at never offering her an explanation. I need not have worried. She and I worked together surprisingly well, untroubled by the past.

A few years after Lisa quit working for me to raise her long-awaited children, she and her husband got divorced. It was the messiest divorce I ever handled, involving adultery on her husband's part, and complicated by my personal relationship with the parties.

Carol's lack of jealousy toward what Lisa and I had once felt for each other astounded me. I'm the very jealous type—if Carol were to see Warren Rogers, even in a doctor-patient relationship, I would be upset. It even upset me when Robert Redford used to come around during election year campaigning for the Democrats and Carol and her friends would go to the rallies to gawk. Carol told me that she wouldn't go if it bothered me. But she had once told me that jealousy was a sign of insecurity, and since I didn't want her to think that I was insecure, I told her that I didn't mind. But I did mind—after all, what did Robert Redford have that I didn't have?

I shook my head at Carol's comment to invite Lisa to work for me. "Lisa's got a good job down there," I said. "She's assistant manager of the supermarket now."

"You can offer to match what the store is paying her," Carol countered. "She's worth it—she already knows the ropes."

"Gas now costs four times more than it did when she was here before. It'd be expensive to commute," I argued.

"Maybe she'd want to move here."

"I doubt it," I replied. "After she got her divorce, I suggested that it might be a good idea to move to Salt Lake or Provo. She'd have a wider range of marriage prospects up there. She told me to mind my own business, and then she said that she needed her family and didn't intend to leave Richfield. I don't think she'd come."

"John, if you need her, she'll come. You know that."

I went into my tiny den and dialed information. The operator gave me the number of Lisa's supermarket, and I dialed it.

"Hello?" a female voice answered. It sounded like Lisa, but I wasn't sure.

"Could I speak to Lisa Johansen, please?"

"Hi, Johnny. This is Lisa."

"Lisa, I'm in a bind up here. My secretary has quit on me with no advance notice. I know you're doing pretty good down there, but Carol suggested that I give you a call and ask you whether you'd maybe consider coming up here and working for me for a while."

"Sure," she said, before I had even told her what wage I could afford to pay her. "Do you want me temporarily, or do you want me permanently?"

"Anyway you want. I'll match what you're making at the supermarket and kick in some extra for gas."

She laughed. She always had a pleasant laugh. "You'd better offer me more than that," she said. "Assistant manager sounds like a big deal, and there're plenty of headaches, but the pay isn't that great. I'll settle for whatever you're paying Alice."

"You were better than Alice. I'll pay you better too."

"Sounds fair enough. You always were a soft touch. But I want to make it clear right now that I'm going to make you buy your own gifts for Carol. I think it's awful how you had Alice buy Carol's gifts. A husband should be the one to pick out things for his wife."

"Alice liked to do it," I replied. "And Carol commented on how much my taste had improved since we were first married. You haven't told Carol that Alice was buying those things, have you?"

"Carol and I don't hide many things from each other, but no, your guilty secret is safe with me."

"When can you start?" I inquired.

"I can't just leave my boss in the lurch, like Alice did to you," she replied. "I'll talk to him. There're a couple of people here who are ready for promotion, so it shouldn't take long. You know of any nice place up there that I can afford to move into?"

"Oh, you want to move here?"

"With unleaded going at the price it is, I can't very well afford to commute. And I don't want to be a long way from my kids in case something happens. Things have changed from when I used to work for you."

"I didn't think you wanted to leave Richfield."

"Would you want to spend the rest of *your* life in Richfield?" she retorted.

I laughed.

"When I got divorced, I needed my folk's emotional support. I think I'm ready to go out on my own again. Can you check with Adney and see if he knows of any nice little place I can afford?"

A thought occurred to me.

"Listen, Lisa, Brother and Sister Reynolds down the street are going on an eighteen-month mission early next month. They've mentioned that they would like a responsible person to move in and take care of the place while they're gone. They're leaving everything and don't want it all ripped up, and they want the yard well taken care of. They said that they'd let someone stay there rent-free if they could find a trustworthy person to take good care of the place. They ought to remember you, and maybe if they haven't found anybody else yet, you could move into their place next month."

"Wonderful! When are they leaving?"

"The first of May. I'll see if I can find a place for you and the kids to stay until they leave."

"Sounds great."

I hesitated a minute. I suddenly felt guilty at trying to get Lisa involved in this. The people wouldn't be any easier on her than they were on Alice. She had already suffered enough because of me.

"Lisa, maybe we'd better forget the whole thing."

"What? Free rent, a boost in salary, good companionship, and you're telling me to forget it?"

"Lisa, I'm handling a murder case. It's pretty dirty business."

"I know. That's OK—I'm a big girl."

"Alice resigned because of a poison pen letter she got from an admirer. I won't be very popular around here for a while. If you come, you're bound to catch my leprosy too."

"Just because you were assigned to defend that Montague guy?" she asked incredulously.

"The victims were pretty popular. But it's going to get worse."

"Why?" she asked.

"I think they'll get off on a technicality."

There was silence on the other end of the line.

"Lisa, I don't know if it's fair to expose you to this."

There was still silence for a moment.

"Johnny, do you need me?"

"I need somebody," I admitted.

"Then I'll come."

Who can find a virtuous woman? for her price is far above rubies. "Thank you, Lisa. Call me after you talk to your boss."

We hung up.

Carol was standing in the doorway. "When's she coming?"

"You're pretty sure of her, aren't you?" I replied.

"I know Lisa, and I've seen the 'Lindsey Family Fortress' in action. Your family always sticks together and presents a united front to the world when one of you is threatened. When's she coming?" she repeated.

"She has to talk to her boss. She'll call back later."

"Did you tell her that the Reynoldses are leaving and she can stay in their house next month?"

"Yeah, I thought of that. I'll check around and see if there's any place we can put them until the Reynoldses leave."

"What's wrong with right here?"

I shook my head. "I'm sure they'd want some privacy."

"With Brenda and Matt gone, we have plenty of room. We can just move Mark and Cindy back in with Paul and Susie, and Lisa and her kids can have the whole basement with their own bathroom—all the privacy they need. I can take care of Sean and Jenny while Lisa's at work. Sean's in school now, so that won't be any trouble at all. Heaven knows she shared her house with you for a long time."

It was obvious that I had already lost the argument before it had even started.

"OK, I'll tell her when she calls back."

Carol sat on my lap and snuggled up next to me. "It'll be nice to have Lisa here again," she remarked. She looked at me for confirmation, but I didn't reply.

As smart as she was, Carol couldn't read my mind. I was gratified to get the help I would need. I couldn't handle the work alone. I was touched by Lisa's willingness to disrupt her life to help me out. But I couldn't get over a wretched feeling that I was going to repay her faithfulness by dragging her into the abyss with me.

Chapter Thirteen

Mark, Paul, and I drove down to Richfield in the truck on Tuesday to pick up Lisa's things and bring them to Ammon. By the time we got to Richfield, Lisa's plethora of relatives had the situation well in hand. All of her furniture had been moved into a big storage shed next to the milking barn on her father's dairy farm. Her clothes and personal effects were already boxed and waiting to be loaded. Ten minutes after we arrived, Lisa gave all her relatives kisses, and we were on our way. Paul and Mark wondered out loud why they had come. Lisa's boy, Sean, was a favorite of Mark's and rode on his lap, while Lisa and her daughter followed us in their Chevette.

I was pleased the next morning at Lisa's performance. I had forgotten what a relief it was to have a completely reliable, efficient, and thorough secretary. Lisa hadn't lost much from the earlier days. When she didn't understand or wasn't sure about something, she had enough sense to. ask me, rather than blunder on and hope she got it right. Unlike many secretaries who made telephone callers feel like they were intruding on the secretaries' time, Lisa had a nice telephone personality that made the caller feel welcome—and having a beautiful secretary never hurt anyone's business. In fact, when the widowers and divorced men of the county learned of Lisa's presence, it was amazing how many of them suddenly developed minor legal problems that brought them to my office. Lisa quickly developed an active social life.

A month ticked by with the malevolence of a hidden time bomb as the date of the trial approached. The all-important pre-trial hearing to determine the admissibility of the prosecutor's evidence was scheduled for the first Friday of May. I was fully prepared and could afford to take Thursday morning off to help Lisa move into the house that Brother and Sister Reynolds had just vacated.

Carol and Lisa were helping me unload the truck at the Reynolds house when Kurt Vanderhoft's Volvo went by. I waved, but he apparently didn't see me. He continued down the street to my house and parked in my driveway. I shouted at him and waved my arms. He noticed me, got back in his car, and came back up the street. He stopped and motioned to me to come to the car. I opened the door to the passenger's side and asked, "What's on your mind, Kurt?"

"I need to talk to you for a few minutes. Privately," he added, looking at Carol and Lisa.

"Can you ladies carry on without me for a little while?" I called.

Carol smiled. "He's good at arranging things like this. I'll bet he called Kurt and told him to come over."

I got into the car, and he drove off. "What's up?" I asked.

"Look, John, I just want to make it clear right now that I didn't have anything to do with this. But Adney Cannest and his family have changed their story about what they saw the night of the arrest. And Frost called from wherever he is and told me a different story from what you said he told you about that night. Like I say, I didn't have anything to do with it."

"Sounds like Frost must have realized what was going on and talked to Adney and his family," I said grimly. "The judge'll have his hide for talking about the case."

"John," he said, not looking at me, "if you try to get that evidence about the wallet and the money thrown out, I'm going to let Adney and Frost speak their pieces."

I turned to him in astonishment. "But you know good and well that Frost told Chief Reitzen and me that he pulled those guys over because they were hippie freaks."

"That's what *you* say," he replied.

"But Chief Reitzen heard it too."

"What you and Chief Reitzen heard was hearsay. Frost and the Cannests were eyewitnesses."

"Hearsay's admissible in the pretrial hearing," I countered.

"True, but it won't stand up against five eyewitnesses."

"Look, you know that Frost and the Cannests are lying. I can't believe you'll use this. And Chief Reitzen doesn't have any reason to lie."

"I'm willing to let the judge decide who's credible and who's lying," Kurt said. "I'm no judge."

"The heck you're not!" I exploded. "The county prosecutor is more of a judge than a real judge. You dispose of more cases every day than any judge. You decide who is to be prosecuted and who is to be released without prosecution. By plea bargaining you decide the degree of punishment that the accused receives. You're in violation of prosecutorial ethics by prosecuting a case you know you can't win, and now you're violating them again by presenting perjured testimony. What's wrong with you? Is the office of attorney general so important to you that you're willing to lie to get there?"

"I'll do my job, and you do yours."

"Pull over."

"I'll drive you home."

"I said pull over!"

He pulled the car to the curb, and I got out, slamming the door behind me. I jogged back to the Reynolds house.

"What did Kurt want?" Carol asked.

"Legal mumbo-jumbo," I replied, shaking my head. I helped unload the truck. Carol wanted me to come in and rearrange the furniture, but I told her I'd do it when I came back. I got into the truck and drove to the courthouse in Manti.

"Is the judge in her office?" I asked Judge Hastings's secretary.

She shook her head. "She's in court right now. The judge is trying to clear the calendar before the hearing tomorrow and the trial Monday."

"When will she be out?"

"I don't know."

"I need to talk to her. It's really important."

"I'll have her call you when she can."

I thanked her and left.

I drove back to Ammon and stopped at the police station. Chief Reitzen wasn't there. I was told he was on patrol at the north end of town. I found his patrol car parked behind a tree. He was pointing his radar gun at the highway.

"How's hunting?" I asked.

"Pretty bad. But as far as I'm concerned, when it's bad it's good. I'd rather have people obey the law than catch them when they don't."

"Heber, the pretrial hearing is tomorrow."

"I know. I'll be there."

"What're you going to say?"

"The truth. What else?"

"What is the truth?" I asked.

A car went by. The radar gun registered 34.

"There goes a speeder," I said.

"I don't bother them unless they break 35," he replied. "I always give them five miles leeway."

"Good for you. What are you going to say tomorrow about the things Frost told us?"

"Just what he said, of course. How he was out to clean up the town, scare away the hippie freaks. How he pulled Montague and Sanchez over because they were long-hairs, and how he frisked them when they talked back."

"OK," I said.

"Why? What's going on?"

"I think Frost has been talking. Kurt says that the Cannests and Frost are changing their tale for tomorrow."

Heber shook his head slowly. "Look," he said quietly, "I know what's going to happen tomorrow as a result of my testimony. I'm a lawman. I'm supposed to protect society from guys like Montague and Sanchez. But because of my testimony, they'll go back into society and kill again. I'm sworn to obey the law, but if I obey the law tomorrow, justice will fall apart. It'll be a joke. But I've got to tell what I saw and heard. I can't do anything but tell the truth."

I left Heber and drove over to the Cannest home. A thought occurred to me before I got out of the car, and I left the Cannests' and drove home. I went upstairs and slipped the tiny tape recorder that Mike Kanagawa had purchased for me in Japan into my front shirt pocket. I drove back to the Cannests' place and rang the doorbell. Sister Cannest answered.

She turned red when she saw me. I asked her if Adney was there. She said he was at the office. I went to his office, but Adney wasn't there. I returned to the Cannest home. Sister Cannest answered the doorbell again.

"Sister Cannest, may I talk to you for a minute?"

She nodded nervously.

"May I come in?"

"I guess so."

I entered the house. She pointed at the couch and I sat down. She sat in a chair clear across the room.

"Your husband wasn't at the office," I said.

"Then I don't know where he is. He leaves a lot."

"Sister Cannest, are you ready to testify at the hearing tomorrow?"

She was silent.

"I've heard a rumor that your husband has decided to change his testimony and that his family is prepared to follow suit. Is that true?"

She stared at the floor, her ears a bright red.

"I'll talk to your husband. I hope I can straighten him out. If I don't, there's a chance that he could spend time in jail. His standing in the Church could be affected too."

"Bishop, what am I going to do?" she suddenly moaned piteously. "I'm supposed to follow my husband."

"Into perjury?" I responded.

She didn't say anything.

"You have an obligation to speak the truth, no matter what the judge does as a result of your testimony."

She barely nodded her head.

"What're you going to say?" I inquired.

"Bishop, I really didn't see that much." Her voice was trembling.

"I know. But like they'll ask you tomorrow, are you going to tell the truth, the whole truth, and nothing but the truth about the things you did see?"

She nodded again.

I left her and drove to Manti High. When the lunch bell rang, I entered the school and waited outside the cafeteria. I said hello to a bunch of the kids I knew, and finally Karen Cannest came by.

"Karen, I need to talk to you for a minute."

She nodded glumly.

After we went outside and I started talking, she began to cry. She was always an easy crier—she could never finish a talk or a testimony without crying. After I talked to her for a few minutes, she tearfully agreed that she would tell the truth.

I drove over to the junior high, or Ephraim Middle School as they call it. When the lunch bell rang, the kids swarmed into the hallway.

"Hi, Bishop!" a voice behind me called out. It was Ted Rendelle, a boy in our ward.

"Hi, Ted. Do you happen to know where Bobby Cannest is?"

"He just got out of P.E. They go around the back way. He's probably already in the cafeteria. I'll help you find him, if you want."

"Thank you, I'd appreciate that."

I followed him into the cafeteria.

"He's right over there, Bishop," Ted pointed out.

Bobby was close to the head of the food line, carrying an empty tray. When he saw me, he looked uncertain for a moment, then resignedly put his tray back in the pile and walked over to meet me.

"Hello, Bishop," he said in a subdued tone.

"Can we go out for a minute?" I asked.

He nodded. We went outside and sat on a raised flower bed.

"Are you ready to testify tomorrow?" I asked.

He shrugged his shoulders.

"Has your dad been talking to you?"

He nodded.

"Are you going to tell the truth?"

He paused for a moment. "I want to, Bishop. But if I do, Dad says that those murderers will go free and kill again."

"It's possible," I replied.

"But I read in the Doctrine and Covenants how we aren't supposed to lie just because we think someone else is also lying," he continued.

"That's right," I replied, a little surprised. I hadn't realized that I had a thirteen-year-old theologian on my hands.

"But Bishop, if those guys go free and they kill again, won't that be my fault?"

"If a doctor sees a man bleeding to death and knows the man is a murderer, but he keeps that man from dying, and later that man kills again, is the doctor a murderer too for saving that guy's life?"

"I don't know. Is he?"

It occurred to me that my hypothetical situation wasn't very close to the point, but it was the first thing I had thought of.

"Bobby, we ought to tell the truth as we see it."

"If the doctor saves the murderer, then whose fault is it if the murderer kills again?" Bobby asked, insistent for an answer.

"I'd say it was the murderer's fault. The doctor did his duty. Just because the doctor did the good thing that he had to do, it wasn't his fault if his patient continued in evil."

"Did the doctor live in our county?" he asked.

"I just made that example up," I said.

"Oh."

"Bobby, are you going to tell the truth tomorrow?"

He squirmed nervously. "Dad'd get pretty darn mad."

"I'm going to talk to your dad," I said. "But I can tell you something: If the Cannest family lies under oath, I wouldn't be a bit surprised to see your dad go to jail. Unless I'm mistaken, someone's probably going to be fined or go to jail tomorrow for contempt of court. Somebody who wasn't supposed to talk told your dad some things he wasn't supposed to. The judge is going to be pretty upset at someone tomorrow. Let's not make it any worse by lying. Chief Reitzen will tell the truth tomorrow, and anybody who lies is going to contradict him. I think the judge will believe him. Don't get yourself in trouble."

He unconsciously pulled a leaf from a flower stem and twisted it between his fingers. He rolled it into a little ball and dropped it on the ground.

"Are you going to tell the truth tomorrow?" I inquired.

"Bishop, isn't killing worse than lying?"

"Yes."

"Then isn't it better for me to lie than to let those guys kill again?"

"Is that something your dad told you, or did you think it up all by yourself?"

"That's what Dad said."

"You tell the truth tomorrow. If there's any killing done, it won't be your responsibility."

"Whose will it be?"

"Look, Bobby, you tell the truth tomorrow. That's where your duty lies."

He nodded his head. I left.

Adney still wasn't in his office when I went by.

I changed into my business suit at home and went to my office. But after reading the same paragraph in *Pacific Reporter* five times without understanding it, I decided to give up. My little private office was too small for effective pacing. I went into the reception room, where Lisa was working on some forms.

"Lisa, I'm not getting anything done. If you need a beast of burden, this would be as good a time as any to go back and rearrange the furniture. I won't be able to help you tonight, I have some appointments at the church."

"Sounds good to me," she replied.

We locked up the office. I drove to my house and changed my clothes.

"What are you doing home?" Carol asked.

"I'm going over to Lisa's to move furniture. I'm sure she would look forward to your expert suggestions."

Carol was one of the world's great arrangers of furniture (at least, she was a great supervisor). She was constantly seeking for that elusive perfect arrangement of tables, chairs, and lamps. It kept her happy and was cheaper than redecorating.

Before we could leave, the phone rang.

"John, the judge can talk to you now," her secretary announced.

"Thanks, Martha." I waited for a moment, then the judge came on.

"Hello," she said crossly.

"Your honor, I think someone has violated the gag order you placed on the Wainsgaard murders."

"What makes you think so?"

"It appears that Frost has changed his story about what happened the night of the murder. And the Cannest family have been talked to. They were going to change their stories too."

There was a pause, then she said, "I can't believe Kurt would do something like that."

"I don't think Kurt did it. I think it was probably Frost, but I can't prove it. Frost knew all the facts and could probably figure out the consequences."

"I'm going to knock some heads off," she promised. "Thank you for calling."

Carol and I walked over to Lisa's house. I played serf until the middle of the afternoon. It kept my thoughts occupied. When my two favorite ladies were temporarily satisfied with the layout of the furniture, I went back to Adney Cannest's office. He was there. I walked right in.

"Hello, John," Adney growled. "What do you want?"

"I understand you've changed your story about the night of the arrest and talked your family into changing their stories."

"Haven't changed a thing. We just realized we had been mistaken about a few things."

"Who talked to you? Was it Frost?"

"Nobody has talked to us. I don't know what you're talking about."

"Don't play games with me, Adney. Somebody has been talking to you, and you've decided to commit perjury."

Adney got angry. "Is winning all you care about? It doesn't seem to make any difference to you whether or not justice is done. Do you want those murderers to go free? I'll bet you do! That way you'll get a reputation as a great lawyer, and you'll be able to raise your fees. But if I have to lie to get those guys put where they belong, I'll do it. They're murderers! Can't you get that through your head? But if you have your way and they go free, they'll murder more innocent people. Lying isn't as bad as murder. The Lord will understand that kind of lie."

I remembered the scripture Bobby had mentioned. "Wo be unto him that lieth to deceive because he supposeth that another lieth to deceive, for such are not exempt from the justice of God!" I quoted angrily.

"Justice? You're talking about justice? You don't care about justice. I know very well that your business has been down, and you're using this to drum up more money and clients for yourself. If there's going to be any justice around here, it isn't going to come from you. I'm going to see that these guys get real justice, even if I have to stretch a point to do it!"

"If you lie under oath, I'll do everything I can to make sure you get convicted of perjury."

"It's just your word against mine. And my wife and kids. And you have an interest in this trial—you're on the defense's side, so no one would believe you."

"If you do that, Adney, I swear you'll go to jail. And what about a bishop's court? Can you face that and its consequences?"

"You can't do that!" he shrieked. "You can't prove any of this! It's your word against mine!"

I reached into my shirt pocket and pulled out the tiny tape

recorder. "Testing, one, two, three. The voices you have just heard belong to John Lindsey and Adney Cannest." I put the tape recorder back in my pocket.

"Perjury's a felony. Maybe a few years in prison would give you time to think about honesty and integrity."

"You hypocrite!" he said in a low voice charged with fury. "Don't you lecture me about integrity! Recording me like that's an invasion of privacy!"

"So sue me." The bells on the door jingled as I left.

I was bluffing, at least about the tape recorder. I had never turned it on.

Though it was a warm afternoon, I was shivering. As I approached Lisa's house, Carol and Lisa waved to me from the porch. I went up and sat next to Carol on the chair swing. She looked at me worriedly. "Are you coming down with something?" she asked.

I shook my head. She snuggled next to me. "You don't feel cold or feverish," she said, putting her hand on my forehead. "Lisa, could you go get a blanket?"

"I'm all right," I protested.

Lisa, as my secretary, knew a lot more about what was going on than Carol did. There was unspoken concern in her eyes as she looked at me. She got up and went inside, coming out a moment later with a big blue blanket.

"I'm OK," I insisted, but the shivering continued. Carol put it around my shoulders and wrapped me up.

"We got a bill from Dr. Rogers today," Carol remarked. "When did you see Dr. Rogers?"

"When I went up to Payson to see Wendy Wainsgaard," I replied.

"You didn't tell me. What was wrong with you?"

"Just a few pains I wanted checked," I said evasively.

"From all the talking this guy does at church, you'd never believe how close-mouthed he is at home," Carol said to Lisa. "Where were you having the pains?" she asked.

"It doesn't matter. Just some psychosomatic stuff."

Carol stared at me. I hadn't told her that I had an ulcer. I am cursed with a martyr's complex and prefer to suffer in silence. If Carol had known about the ulcer, she would have started asking more questions, and I wouldn't have been able to answer her. I preferred to just keep quiet about the whole thing.

"Maybe you'd better tell her," Lisa said. "Or if you don't, I will. He's pregnant, Carol. He was going to surprise you."

Carol smiled. "Well, that explains a lot. But I need to know—am I the mother?"

I grinned. The shaking subsided. I took the blanket off.

"What's for dinner?" I asked, hoping to change the subject.

"I've got hamburger thawed out. I was planning on a macaroni casserole. Would you prefer tacos?" Carol asked sympathetically.

"Sure. We got tomatoes?"

"Seventy-nine cents a pound," she replied. "But I can go get some, if you want."

"At that price I can eat tacos without tomatoes."

The school bus pulled up at the corner, and a bunch of kids got out. Sean and Susie came running up to the porch. They both gave their mothers hugs.

"How many tacos do you feel like?" Carol asked me.

"A dozen or so." I stood up with her and gave her a little hug before she went. With one arm carrying Johnny, she and Susie walked down the porch stairs to the sidewalk.

"Carol, let Johnny walk," I said. "He'll never be a good walker if he isn't forced to walk by himself."

Carol sat Johnny down. He wailed for a minute, lifting his arms to indicate that he wanted to be carried. Carol walked slowly down the sidewalk. After he was convinced that he would not be carried, he unsteadily toddled down the sidewalk after Carol.

"Did you see the poison pen letter I got in the mail?" Lisa asked, still sitting on the swing. She handed it to me. It manifested the same spirit of love as did the letter that had driven Mrs. Henderson out of town.

"Are you going to pack up and leave now, like Alice did?" I asked.

"Quit being melodramatic, Johnny," she replied. "Did you withdraw from handling my divorce when it started getting nasty? Besides, I'm developing too many ties here to just pull up and leave."

"Oh? Are you and Leonard getting serious?" Leonard Jones was a recently widowed professor at Snow College with whom Lisa had been spending a lot of time recently.

"He's a neat guy, Johnny," she replied.

"Has he given you any gas over the fact that your boss defends accused murderers?"

"He asked about it," Lisa admitted. "I told him that somebody had to defend the guy, and the court appointed you to do it. He hasn't brought up the subject again."

We were silent for a moment. She brushed a spot of rust off the chain holding up the chair swing. "Why didn't you tell Carol that you have an ulcer?" she asked suddenly.

I looked at her wonderingly. "How did you know?"

"Because I had one myself before I finally divorced Mitch. And Carol mentioned how your milk bill has doubled recently because you've been guzzling so much. I've seen all those little cartons in your wastebasket. And most important I saw the ulcer diet in your top desk drawer when I went to borrow an eraser. You shouldn't be eating deep-fried, spicy things like tacos. Why don't you have Carol fix you things that won't hurt you?"

"This trial will be over next week. I'm sure my ulcer will go with it. No sense getting Carol upset."

"She doesn't know a thing about what's going on, does she?" Lisa asked. "As far as she knows, this is just another case, maybe a little more unpleasant than the rest but just another case."

"There's nothing I can tell her about this case," I replied.

"But that's not any reason to risk damaging yourself with an ulcer. Even after my divorce, it took me a while to get rid of mine. Why are you always so stupid about things like this, Johnny? You pride yourself on how good you take care of your body—you run ten miles a week and work out at the gym on the weights—then you do something like this that can really hurt you. Are you being macho, or what? I remember when you came back from Vietnam. Almost killed by that bullet through your guts, and yet just as soon as they released you from the hospital, you headed out to your brother's job and started carrying wooden beams. You didn't need money that bad. And later you passed out—almost got killed."

"That was the hepatitis that made me pass out, not the wound. I didn't know that I'd caught a bad lot of blood."

"But you knew before you went to work that day that you were sick, even if you didn't know it was hepatitis. And yet you never learn! Here you have an ulcer, and yet you won't do anything about it—you're going to pig out on tacos. You won't even tell your wife. Carol can take bad news. She survived two notices from the Marine Corps, and Johnny Jacob's death. You say the ulcer will go away after next week when the trial's over. How do you know? I wish you'd grow up, Johnny."

"I'll be OK. After the trial, I'll tell Carol. She'll understand then. She has no idea now what's going on, and I want to keep it that way. After the trial, I'll get this cleared up."

Lisa looked at me in exasperation. She didn't say anything for a while. Suddenly, she laughed. "Twelve tacos!" She shook her head. Her anger was fading away. "If I hadn't seen your appetite, I would never have believed it. Fourteen burritos last Saturday night, and then a big pot of popcorn later on when you turned on the TV. If I ate one-fourth that much, I'd look like a blimp." She smiled. "I remember when you used to live with us. We had hot dogs one night, and you took yours and split them down the middle. Then you wrapped each half in bread and ate it. That's one of my earliest memories."

"Well," I explained, "in my house we were allowed all the bread we wanted. When we had hot dogs, I was allowed two. So I'd split them down the middle and put each half in a piece of bread, and it seemed like I had four. But how can you remember that? You were how old? Two or three?"

"Three, I think. The reason I remember it so well is that,

from then on, whenever I wouldn't eat everything on my plate, my folks reminded me about Johnny. Every normal family gets their kids to eat by telling them about the starving kids in India. Instead, my folks always told me about poor little Johnny. I ate a lot of squash and broccoli in your memory." She looked worried for a second. "It doesn't bother you to talk about it, does it? I can be so tactless sometimes."

"It doesn't bother me," I replied. "We weren't poor. We kids just thought we were. We were a lower middle-class family in an upper middle-class neighborhood. But we got by."

"Now you're a rich, successful attorney, and yet I had to laugh a few weeks ago when I saw you slice that hot dog in half," she continued.

"Why not? Carbohydrates are easier to digest than meat. Americans eat too much meat anyway. And I'm not a rich attorney. I did really well my first few years, but now I give the ward members a lot of free advice. You can't have the members worried that everytime they approach their bishop with a problem, they're going to get billed. If I'd stayed in the Marines, with my combat record and my abilities, I'd be a lieutenant colonel by now, maybe even a bird colonel. Even as a major I'd be making more money than I am as an attorney.

"Or I could've become my brother's partner in construction like he wanted me to, instead of going to law school. Even in this building slump he makes three times what I do. During the booms he was clearing a quarter million a year."

"'For of all sad words of tongue and pen, / The saddest are these, "It might have been!"'" she quoted. "Are you sorry that you became a lawyer?"

"Until recently I enjoyed it, in spite of the fact that the big bucks aren't there. Sure, I'd like to be rich—who wouldn't? But today I threatened to get Adney Cannest convicted unless he helped me set a murderer free."

Lisa looked at me with surprise.

"Lisa, what am I going to do?" I said miserably, my voice trembling. "I love the Lord, and I've always done my best to serve him and keep his commandments. I love my country, and I've tried to serve it. As a citizen I'm supposed to be law-abiding, but when I became an attorney, it went further—I took an oath to obey the laws. As far as I'm concerned, my oath has limitations. I will not obey a corrupt, immoral law, like the anti-Semitic Nuremberg laws of the 1930s. I don't believe in blind obedience. But no matter what I might think of the exclusionary rule, it wasn't designed as a corrupt, oppressive law. It was made by well-intentioned men who saw a need and fashioned a remedy to try to cure it. I don't like the rule anymore than I like the income tax laws or the fifty-five-mile-per-hour speed limit. But I can't selectively obey only the laws I enjoy. Grandpa J. J. went to prison rather than submit to a law that conflicted with the Lord's law, and I would do the same now if the Lord required it. But unless the Lord directs otherwise, it is my duty to obey the law. 'Be subject to the powers that be, until he reigns whose right it is to reign.' But it's tearing me apart, Lisa."

There was a long silence. Finally, I turned to walk down the stairs.

"Johnny?"

I looked back.

"When I was a girl in Sunday School, they had us memorize a scripture. 'All things shall work together for good to them that walk uprightly.' "

I made no reply and walked away.

Chapter Fourteen

The pretrial hearing on Friday morning was devoid of drama. Ralph Hersh, the attorney for Bryan Sanchez, woke me up at 5:30 that morning to tell me that he was in town and wanted to hold a strategy meeting. Hersh irritated me. This was only the second time he had even seen his client. The first time he'd flown up he had brushed aside any efforts of mine to plan a combined strategy. He was willing to take advantage of my detective work and let me handle the whole case, while he sat back and collected his fat fee. In my opinion, Hersh simply wasn't acting in his client's best interests. Had I been Sanchez's attorney, I would have hit up Kurt for immunity for my client in return for his testimony against Montague. Had Kurt been aware that Sanchez was not involved in the murders, he probably would have welcomed giving Sanchez immunity from prosecution, saving the case and his own political hide. Though it were true that Sanchez would almost certainly be acquitted in the trial anyway, to the public it would appear that Sanchez was a murderer who escaped punishment by a formality of law. The shadow of murder would follow him for the rest of his life. If I were in Sanchez's position, I would admit my complicity in the robbery and clear my name of the stain of murder. In the process, I would help put away a dangerous criminal and thus pay back in part my debt to society.

Hersh came to my house, and I fixed us breakfast rather

than wake Carol. We discussed the case, and he was satisfied with the way things were going. At nine, we went to the courthouse and met our clients. A few reporters were there, who were upset to learn that they wouldn't be allowed in the courtroom during the hearing.

Sister Cannest was the first witness called. She wasn't good for much except to establish the time of arrest. Karen was sworn in next but burst into tears when she was asked the first question. We managed to calm her down a little, but shortly after she began her story, she started crying again. I let her take her seat.

Bobby was impressive. He was white-faced and obviously frightened, but in a steady voice he told the entire story. Kurt had not cross-examined Sister Cannest, but he attacked Bobby.

"Tell me, Robert," Kurt said, "isn't it true that you disliked Officer Frost before you even met him?"

"What do you mean?"

"I understand that you'd heard about Frost before you ever met him. Officer Frost had allegedly bothered a few of your friends, and you didn't care for the fellow. Isn't that true?"

Bobby nodded. "Yes sir, you see . . ."

"A yes is sufficient. Isn't it possible that you allowed your negative feelings toward Officer Frost to color your recollections of the evening of the arrest in order to get Officer Frost in trouble?"

"No sir."

"No? But you admit that you had developed a prejudicial attitude against Officer Frost before you met him. And now, after admitting your prejudice, you're trying to tell us that it didn't in the least influence your story?"

"No sir," he repeated.

Kurt harped on him some more until I objected and the judge told him to lay off. When Kurt had finished, on redirect I had Bobby tell the story that had caused him to dislike Frost in the first place, where Frost had pulled over my son and three friends to harass them about their hair. I told Judge Hastings

130

that I could have all four boys here in fifteen minutes if she wanted to hear a firsthand account of the incident. She replied that it wouldn't be necessary.

Adney Cannest was not called on to testify. I felt that Bobby and his mother had done a sufficient job of establishing our case. Adney might get on the stand and say something that he would later regret.

Chief Reitzen told his story, though admittedly it was all hearsay on his part. The judge's face registered her displeasure at Frost's blatant abuse of police powers.

Kurt did not call Frost to the stand, though he was present. In spite of what Kurt had told me Thursday morning, he was not about to suborn perjury. But Frost did not escape unscathed. After an investigation later on by Judge Hastings, she fined him $500 and sent him to jail for a weekend for violating her gag order.

As I expected, Judge Hastings ruled that an illegal search and seizure had indeed taken place and that the wallet and money wouldn't be admissible as evidence in the upcoming trial.

Montague and Sanchez had big smiles on their faces when the judge issued her ruling. When the hearing was over, Montague leaned over to me. "That's it, isn't it?" he said. "We're going to go free, aren't we?"

I didn't reply.

"See, Bishop," he said, smiling contemptuously, "you're on the wrong side. I'm going to win, and you're going to lose."

"Montague, we've still got a trial next week. This hearing has pretty much made that trial into a farce. The prosecution doesn't have much to go on. Personally, I don't think what the prosecution has can possibly justify a guilty verdict. But I could be wrong. If I were you, I wouldn't start crowing until the trial is over."

He nodded, grinning. "Sure, Bishop. I don't want to upset you yet. You might get ticked enough to throw the case." He looked over at Sanchez and Hersh, who were talking in low voices. "Bishop, can't you get me a suit to wear at the trial? Bryan's attorney got him one. I look terrible in prison grey."

"Bryan's folks brought him that suit. The court doesn't reimburse me for your wearing apparel. If you give me the bucks, I'll get you a suit. Otherwise, blow it out your ear."

"You don't like me much, do you, Bishop?" He grinned. "Haven't you read that scripture about loving your enemy?"

I stood up and went home.

During my church meetings the next Sunday, I wasn't a particularly effective leader. I allowed thoughts of the trial to preoccupy me. I couldn't help it. My counselors and the other ward leaders must have noticed my preoccupation, but no one said anything.

I made an effort to put my problems away and buckle down in order to fulfill my religious duties, but I found that I was just too tied up in my own troubles to accomplish much. I canceled my remaining appointments and went home. For the first time in years I was home in the middle of the afternoon. I went to my room to read but couldn't find anything that appealed to me. I finally took Johnny out for a walk.

We brought along some carrots to feed to the horses that were stabled nearby. Johnny offered a carrot to a horse that nibbled on it until Johnny jerked it away. He then proceeded to chew on the carrot himself while I wondered how many horse diseases were communicable to humans. He again offered the carrot to the horse and started crying when the horse pulled the carrot from his hands. He was perfectly willing to share, but the horse was a glutton. I gave Johnny another carrot to quiet him, and we walked away from the horses while he chewed on the carrot. He pointed out dogs, birds, trees, and bushes as we strolled along.

When we came to the foot of the mountain at the end of our street, we slowly climbed up the path. Though we took frequent rests, Johnny got tired and discouraged before we reached our goal, so I carried him on the final part of the trail. I sat on a warm rock at the family knoll while Johnny squatted on the ground. I watched patiently as he arranged little designs of bark and twigs in the dust. He whimpered a little every time the breeze scattered his accomplishments. I invited him to come sit in the lee of the big rock I was sitting on, which would have protected him and his efforts from the wind. But he ignored me until a big gust of wind blew dust in his eyes. He whined as he rubbed his eyes, then blindly put his hand on a burr and let out a real wail. I set him on my lap and removed the burr that pricked his skin. He blubbered for a little while but stopped when a huge blue dragonfly lit on our rock, within temptingly easy reach of his little hands. He quietly watched it awhile, then reached out to grasp it. I stopped him before he touched it. The dragonfly sat motionless for a moment longer, then flew off. I watched the sun set, then carried him back down the trail.

I went to bed early that night, hoping for the oblivion of sleep. But though I finally managed to doze off, I slept fitfully, tossing and turning so much that it disturbed Carol's rest. At half past three, I finally gave up. I put on my robe and went outside. In our backyard were three English walnut trees that I had planted when we first moved to Ammon. I had built an octagonal white bench around one of them. I sat on the bench and watched the stars.

The sky was grey with the coming dawn when I heard the back door open, then the quiet swish of slippered feet. A tender hand brushed my cheek. I took Carol's hand and pulled her down onto my lap.

"Looking for worms, early bird?" she asked softly.

I didn't reply. I held her silently as the two of us watched the sunrise.

Chapter Fifteen

I was surprised to find plenty of parking at the courthouse that morning. I had expected to be mobbed by reporters and television crews, but apparently a remote county like ours was not worthy of news coverage. I parked my car, grabbed my briefcase, and walked briskly to the courthouse.

The Manti courthouse, built during the depression as a WPA make-work project, had all the architectural grace of an orange crate. It was a big stone building, built of cream-colored rock from the same quarry that had supplied stone for the Manti Temple more than fifty years earlier. It held all of the Sanpete County offices, including the sheriff's office and the county jail in the basement. Montague and Sanchez had been transferred from the Richfield jail for the duration of the trial back to our tiny structure.

Sticking out from the wall on both sides of the courthouse entrance were huge, grotesque bronze lamps. Underneath one of the lamps, an exceptionally beautiful young woman was standing with her arms folded. I couldn't recall seeing her before, but when she saw me, she unfolded her arms and smiled at me. The smile was too big to denote mere friendliness. As I approached the front door, she moved in front of me.

"Excuse me . . ." she began, but I brushed past her. I wasn't interested in reporters. As I entered the lobby, a man's voice cried out, "Mr. Lindsey, look what you're doing to my floor!"

It was Mr. Jergens, the building's custodian. I looked down. My briefcase was dripping milk. I was too cheap to pay forty cents for the tiny cartons of milk from the vending machine, so I had brought my own in a Thermos that had sprung a leak.

"I tried to tell him when he came in," the beautiful girl remarked.

I took my briefcase outside and set it in the bushes. I went in and got some paper towels from the men's room. Blushing deeply, I wiped up the milk before Mr. Jergens reappeared with his mop. After I finished, I checked the papers in my briefcase—they were soaked. It was an auspicious beginning.

Ralph Hersh joined me in the office of the county agricultural agent, who had kindly evacuated it so that the defense attorneys would have a convenient base of operations for the trial. Hersh said he wanted to take charge of questioning the prospective jurors. I explained that in Utah the judge did the direct questioning, and that our main part in the selection process was to suggest questions for the judge to ask. In a sensitive, well publicized case like ours, we would probably be allowed great latitude in the range of our questions. Hersh told me that with his considerable experience in criminal trials, he felt better qualified than I to pick the kind of jurors we were after. I agreed, then asked him if he wanted to go home with me at lunchtime for hog jowls and grits.

Judge Hastings had wisely provided an extraordinarily large number of people from which to choose our jury. Because of the huge size of our judicial district, some had driven 200 miles to the courthouse. There were 116 audience seats in the courtroom in addition to the jury seats, but so many had been called for jury duty that some people had to stand.

As we were beginning, a troupe of reporters filed in with their usual air that this trial was being staged especially for their benefit. Judge Hastings threw them out. When one of them grandiloquently vowed to appeal to the highest courts, Judge Hastings said fine, that by the time the appeals were through she'd have time to pare this group down to make room for the press.

The crowd was quickly reduced to manageable proportions, and the judge invited the reporters back in. She excused anyone who had known the victims or any of the attorneys involved, and that got rid of all but two of the Sanpete County residents as well as a healthy proportion from Sevier County. Of the fifty-two people left, all but two admitted having heard or read about the case. Hersh whispered that we'd better ask for a new venire in order to find some people who were completely untainted with knowledge of the case. I replied that anyone who claimed he hadn't heard or read about the case was either an illiterate deaf-mute or a liar, and I didn't care for either type on my juries. Most of those who had heard about the murder said that they could judge the case solely on the basis of evidence presented in trial. Hersh didn't like it, though it sounded fair enough to me. But then, us naive country boys will trust anybody.

After the number had been pared down to forty-five, the examinations went slowly. We broke for lunch, returned, and crawled through the questioning for the rest of the afternoon. When Judge Hastings sent us home for the day, the jury selection process was still incomplete.

At home that night, it was my turn to conduct family home evening, but I begged off and Carol pinch-hit for me. I was tense, edgy, and hard put to keep from snapping at the kids. After family home evening, with my self-control stretched thin, I banished myself to my bedroom. I was so tired from lack of sleep the previous night that I eventually drifted off to sleep, fully dressed.

I awoke at dawn, with Carol asleep beside me. My vest and suit pants were badly wrinkled. It occurred to me that my other suit was at the cleaners. I had another pair of pants to match my suit coat, but I'd have to go without a vest today.

We dragged through some more jury selection that morning and finally finished examining the panel. We then proceeded to use our peremptory challenges to get down to our final twelve jurors, with two alternate jurors in case someone got sick or had to be excused during the course of the trial.

Hersh was really in his element now and showed me how they do things in the big city.

Eight women and four men were finally chosen, with a man and a woman alternate. The judge let us go for lunch, even though it was only a few minutes after eleven. With the extra time, I drove back to Ammon and picked up my other suit from Li's cleaners, then went home for lunch.

Carol was subdued when I got home. She fed me, then unexpectedly sat next to me and laid her head on my shoulder. "Sweetheart, what's the matter?" she asked. "I know something's happening to you, and I want to help."

I shook my head as I always do when responding to questions concerning things I wasn't allowed to talk about.

"That's not good enough this time, John. You've shaken your head at me ever since you became a lawyer, and now that you're a bishop it's even worse. But I'm not accepting it this time. I see you barely controlling yourself about things that usually don't bother you. I appreciate your control, but it's giving you a nervous tic, and I want to know what's going on."

"I have a tic?"

"The left corner of your mouth twitches a lot now. Something's tearing you apart, and your secretary knows about it, but your wife doesn't. Tell me so I can help."

Her earnestness touched me—part of the problem was that I couldn't tell her. "I'm sorry, Carol. A bishop's counselors know a lot of things that a bishop's wife doesn't get to know, and a lawyer's secretary hears a lot of things that his wife never hears. I know it's not fair to you. But as long as I'm a bishop and an attorney, there'll be holes in our conversation."

"John, the only thing I can figure out is that you believe your client is innocent, but all the evidence is against him. He's going to be punished for something he didn't do, and you're frustrated because you can't help him. Is that right?"

I exploded into bitter laughter. I pulled Carol close and hugged her.

"Then that's it, isn't it?" she concluded.

I realized that Carol had such a high opinion of me that it would never occur to her that I might be setting a murderer free until she was forced after the event to confront the fact. I hoped that by the end of the week I would still have her love, if not her understanding.

"Darling, you've been reading too much of *To Kill a Mockingbird.* It helps to know that you're concerned. I wish I could tell you, but I can't. I wish I could ease your mind, but anything I told you would only make matters worse. You'll have to wait for your information like everyone else."

"Well, at least I know you well enough to be certain that whatever you're doing is the right thing," she said.

I wished I had her certainty.

When the trial resumed later that afternoon, Kurt gave his opening remarks, telling the jury the things he would prove. For an obese man, he had graceful movements that emphasized the points he wanted to get across. But considering how little evidence he had, his opening statement took a long time. After he finished, I made the opening statements for the defense. I kept them short, and I'm sure the jury appreciated it.

Though we only used half the afternoon, Judge Hastings sent us home. Kurt could have presented most of the prosecution's evidence in the time remaining. Not even he could make soup from a stone.

At home I made the mistake of wondering out loud what I could do for the rest of the day. Carol, ever helpful, wrote me a list. I spent the rest of the day cleaning the oven, defrosting the freezer, replacing the washers on the faucets, and preparing the swamp cooler for the coming summer. When I knelt on the floor with my head in the oven, I jokingly asked Carol to turn on the gas. She got really angry and said I wasn't being funny.

That night passed relatively well. I guess a person can get used to anything.

I picked Lisa up at her house the next morning. The answering machine would have to hold the fort today because I needed her to assist Professor Fields and to run errands.

"Good morning," she said as she got in the car. "Are you going to be needing me all day tomorrow too?" she asked.

I shook my head. "We ought to finish today."

She looked a little surprised. "One day, for a capital case?"

I nodded.

She looked out the window and gazed at the sky. There were only a few fluffy cumulus clouds spotting up the blue of the heavens, and it was supposed to get up to the high seventies by the afternoon.

"It's going to be a beautiful day," she remarked.

"Yes, it is—a great day for setting a murderer free."

She didn't speak again as the scenery rushed by.

A mob of reporters, just as pushy and rude as they are in the movies, stood at the courthouse door.

I ignored them, or at least I tried to. I saw Jerry Newcarter, but surprisingly he wasn't being obnoxious. He just smiled and said, "Hi, Johnny."

I nodded back.

I met Montague in the courtroom. "You think I'll be a free man by tomorrow night?" he asked, leaning back in his chair and putting his hands behind his head in a gesture of total ease and unconcern. He was enjoying himself.

"We ought to finish today, unless Kurt gets long-winded again. But then, the jury might take a while to deliberate. But I'm not sure about you getting released because I can't be absolutely sure what the jury's verdict will be."

He laughed. He knew that I was pretty darn sure what the jury would decide. And if the jury didn't free him, Judge Hastings probably would arrest the judgment. And we still had the Utah Supreme Court and the federal court system. As I saw it, Montague would eventually go free.

When Kurt led Wendy Wainsgaard in, I exploded. She had a bandage around her head. Kurt was helping her sit down when I grabbed him from behind by the shoulder and whirled him around. "What's going on here, Kurt? Are you turning this whole thing into a circus? She didn't have any bandages on her head the last time I saw her!"

When he saw my anger, he got angry himself. "I notice that Montague and Sanchez aren't the long-haired hippies they were four months ago either!" he retorted.

"The jail shaved them and gave them haircuts. You know that."

"And newly blind people get disoriented a lot and fall down," he responded. "She cut her head on a kitchen cabinet. You want to see the stitches?"

"I sure do."

"Wendy," he said gently, "I need to take your bandage off for a minute, OK?"

"Yes, sir," she replied.

"Don't bother, I believe you," I said, but I was still angry.

"What's wrong with you?" he asked acidly. "I can't believe how paranoid you're getting."

"If everyone were out to get you, you'd be paranoid too."

He must have thought that I was trying to be funny, because his features softened and he chuckled. I left him and went back to the defense table.

"Why the makeup on the retard?" Hersh asked me.

"She fell and cut her head. Stitches and everything."

"Sure. I'll bet."

"Check it out, if you want to," I responded.

"Aw, forget it. You're going to cut her to pieces anyway. That little getup might inflame the jury, but they got nothing on our clients," he said confidently. "Just gives us more grounds for appeal if something goes wrong and we lose. You got a camera to take a picture of the moron and her bandages?"

"Not on me."

"Well, then send your secretary home for one. It might tend to show passion and prejudice in an appeal."

"Not now," I replied. "Maybe at lunchtime."

We were all called to attention and stood up as the judge entered. After the opening formalities, Wendy Wainsgaard was called to the stand.

"Do you solemnly swear that the testimony you give shall be the truth, the whole truth, and nothing but the truth?"

She looked confused. "Swear words are bad," she said finally.

The clerk automatically asked her if she solemnly *affirmed* that she would tell the truth, the whole truth, and nothing but the truth. Wendy still looked confused. Hersh, Montague, and Sanchez grinned.

The judge swiftly intervened. "Wendy, do you promise to tell us the truth?"

"Yes, ma'am."

"Thank you, Wendy. You may proceed, Mr. Vanderhoft."

I had challenged Wendy's competency to testify in a pretrial motion, but the judge denied it. Her inability to grasp the simple swearing-in made an impression on the jury.

A mentally handicapped person often has a certain indefinable look that exposes his or her mental deficiency. Wendy had no congenital physical handicaps, but she looked as if her face had been molded in clay and then been slightly squashed. I understood that she had helped her mother well in the dry cleaning business, and she was polite and correct in her actions, but that was due to good training rather than to any intelligence. She did as she was told, and fortunately she had always been told to do good.

Kurt led her into her testimony about the events of the murder. She talked in a slow, careful, well-drilled voice.

"The doorbell rang, and I answered it, and it was Brother Coombs. He told me 'Merry Christmas,' and he gave me a present. I opened it, and it was peanut brittle. I ate a piece, and Mom came in and I gave her a piece, and she ate it. It was good. Mom said come in, and she gave us both some cocoa. Mom asked him why didn't he bring his kids, and he said how they'd been in Mount Pleasant all day and the kids were all wore out. At their grandpa's. And then Mom said how Sister Coombs's sweater was ready, and did he want to take it home. So we went into the shop . . ."

"Is the shop part of the house?" Kurt interrupted.

She nodded. "The front part by the driveway. It used to be the garage. But Robert and Mark, they made it into the shop."

"After your father passed away?"

"What?"

"After your father died?"

"What after my father died?"

"Is that when you opened the shop?"

She looked confused. Kurt apparently hadn't coached her on this part; he was just throwing it in for pathos. But he had messed up her recording, so he hurriedly got her back on the right track. "Please continue," he said. Long narrative is not the normal examination method, but we let it go.

"What?"

"What happened after you went into the shop?"

"Well, I turned on the light. And then I looked for the Cs. *Coombs* is *C* not *K*. And I got the sweater. It was white and kind of furry. And kind of blue at the top. Maybe not blue, kind of dark blue but kind of purple a little bit . . ."

"What happened after you got the sweater?"

"There was some knocking on the front door. I went—"

"A knock on the shop front door or the house?"

"What?"

"Was there a knock on the shop front door?"

"Yes. That's what I said. I opened it, and two guys came in. One guy had a gun, and he wanted money, and he told us to get on the floor. But not Mom. He told Mom to get him some money, and she opened the cash register and gave him some. But he wanted more. So she got some out of the closet, and I watched her, and some of that money was mine, but he took it all. And then he made us get on our tummies. And that's all I remember."

"What happened to the sweater?"

"I don't know. Maybe he stole it too."

Kurt then proceeded to introduce the bloody sweater into evidence. I objected, saying that it was just intended to create passion and prejudice in the jury. The judge overruled me. Kurt waved the bloody sweater for a moment, like a Civil War carpetbagger, and then set it down.

"Tell me, Wendy, what did the men look like?"

"Well, Brother Coombs was kind of skinny, and he had—"

"Not Mr. Coombs. Tell us what the bad men looked like."

"Oh, you mean the stuff about the light and dark, like you said," she stated innocently. Kurt flushed, and Hersh joyously jabbed me in the ribs with his elbow. The jury couldn't help but notice this evidence of coaching.

"Well, one of them was light, and one was dark," she continued. "And one of them had a beard, and one of them didn't. And one of them had blue eyes, and the other one had brown eyes. And one of them had really long hair, and the other one had not so long hair. And one of them was tall, and the other one was short—"

"Excuse me, Wendy," Kurt said hurriedly, and this time it was Montague who happily poked me in the ribs. Wendy had gotten carried away in her list of opposites.

Kurt was a quick thinker and acted as if the cutoff were a deliberate part of his presentation. "I would like to introduce into evidence at this point photographs of the defendants taken the day after the murders." He passed to the jury blown-up mug shots of Sanchez and Montague that clearly showed that Sanchez had been clean-shaven while Montague had had a beard, and that Montague's hair had been considerably longer than Sanchez's. He then passed out color photographs showing Montague's light blue eyes and light features and Sanchez's dark features and brown eyes. Then Kurt asked the court's permission to perform a little demonstration. He wanted Montague and Sanchez to read something so that Wendy could identify them by voice. I motioned to Lisa, whispered in her ear, and sent her out. Hersh didn't like the thought of having our clients talk, but I told him that I was ready for it. He decided that it would look worse for our clients to refuse to speak. Our clients stood up, and Kurt handed them both pieces of paper. Montague looked at his and smiled. He put his hand over his heart and said in a clear, deeply sincere voice, "I pledge allegiance to the flag of the United States of America and to the republic for which it stands, one nation under God, indivisible, with liberty and justice for all." Sanchez said the same thing. I wondered why Kurt chose that for the defendants to recite.

Kurt asked Wendy if those were the voices of the men who had entered the shop and robbed them. She said they were. Kurt turned her over to me for cross-examination.

"Chew that retard up and spit her out!" Hersh whispered to me.

My voice was kind and my manner polite as I asked Wendy some questions. She had testified that one of the men in the shop was tall and that one was short. I asked her if that were true. She got confused. I asked the court reporter to repeat her words on the subject.

"And one of them was tall, and the other one was short," he read back. I asked Wendy if that were what she remembered. She was still confused.

I asked the court's indulgence: since the prosecutor had asked the defendants to stand, could the defense do the same? I had them take off their shoes and stand back to back. They were both the same size.

I then asked the judge if I could continue the prosecution's demonstration. She agreed. I had the court bailiff, Montague, a news reporter, and a deputy sheriff repeat the Pledge of Allegiance. I mentioned to Wendy that she had identified the bad guy by his voice and asked whether his voice were among the four she had just heard. She wasn't sure. I pressed her and had them repeat it again. She chose the reporter. We went through the demonstration again, and she chose Montague. The third time, she chose the reporter again, and the fourth time she also chose the reporter.

"You've made your point, Mr. Lindsey, please continue." the judge said.

I was stalling, wondering where Lisa was. I picked three other spectators and had them read the Pledge of Allegiance with Sanchez. When asked to identify the bad guy, she picked Sanchez. I stalled for a few minutes until Lisa came back in, accompanied by Bishop Alvirez. He was dressed in his police uniform. Bishop Alvirez was a natural-born American through his mother, but because of his background he had just the slightest flavor of a Mexican accent, like Bryan Sanchez had. Other than the slight accent, their voices were nothing alike.

This time, I excluded Sanchez and had Bishop Alvirez and three others repeat the Pledge of Allegiance. I asked Wendy if she recognized the voice of the bad guy. She chose Bishop Alvirez. I next had Bishop Alvirez, Sanchez, and two others repeat the pledge again. After a brief hesitation, she again chose Bishop Alvirez, and twice more repeated her error.

"Sorry, Bishop, guilty as charged," I said, and the jury and spectators laughed.

Kurt declined any redirect and called Chief Reitzen to the stand. Chief Reitzen testified briefly about the events of the night. The most salient fact that he established was that Montague had been arrested in a dark green Mustang. Montague was the registered owner of the vehicle. Kurt thanked him, and I declined to question him. Kurt called his next witness.

Karen Shears was a woman in her late fifties who was a neighbor of the Wainsgaards. Though I hadn't known her by name, I had seen her before in connection with the *Mormon Miracle Pageant* that our valley put on each summer.

Kurt asked Mrs. Shears about her movements the night of the murders. Like the Coombs, she had been visiting relatives that Christmas day, and she was delivering belated gifts that night to her neighbors. She testified that as she passed the Wainsgaard house, she noticed a dark green Mustang parked nearby. When she said that, I noticed a pain starting to grow in my stomach. It didn't fade away.

"I wondered who was visiting the Wainsgaards," she said, "because I didn't know anyone with a dark green Mustang. I went to a neighbor's house to give them a present and sat and talked for a while. When I went back outside, I noticed that the dark green Mustang was gone. Since I intended to give the Wainsgaards a present too, I rang their front doorbell. No one answered. I thought, from the lights in the shop, that the

Wainsgaards must be working on some rush job, so I went to the shop entrance. I saw some still figures on the floor. The door was locked, so I went home and called the police."

"It was nighttime, Mrs. Shears," Kurt said. "How could you tell that there was a dark green Mustang in front? Was there a streetlight, or did a car go past, or were there outside lights on?"

"No, but it wasn't dark," she replied. "The moon was almost full. And there was snow on the ground, so it was really bright."

Kurt introduced evidence showing that the moon had indeed been almost full that night and that it had been a cloudless evening. Kurt finished, and I approached the witness.

"Hello, Mrs. Shears," I said.

"Hello, Bishop Lindsey," she replied. For a reason unknown to me, a jurywoman suddenly burst into a smile.

"Mrs. Shears, we have all heard you testify that a Ford Mustang was parked close to the Wainsgaard house. How do you know it was a Ford Mustang?"

"There're lots of Mustangs around. Everyone knows what a Mustang looks like," she replied.

I nodded my head. "There are indeed a lot of Mustangs around. It was for a while the best-selling car in America, so they're plentiful, just like you say. But there're a few things I'd like to discuss with you. You testified today that you saw a dark green Mustang parked by the Wainsgaards'. When I talked to you several months ago, you said that there was a dark green Mustang there. And when Mr. Vanderhoft talked to you, you told him the same thing. Is that right?"

"Yes, it is."

"The night of the murder, two reports were written that say you told the police and the sheriff that the car was a dark-colored Mustang. You didn't say dark green, you said dark *colored*," I emphasized. "Was it dark green, or dark colored?"

"It was dark colored, dark green colored," she replied.

"Then that night, when it was so important to the authorities to have as accurate a description as possible so that they would know exactly what to look for, why didn't you tell them that it was dark green? You told the police that it was dark colored, you told the sheriff that it was dark colored, so the APB that went out described it as dark colored. There're plenty of dark-colored Mustangs around, so why weren't you more exact? *Dark green* is much more exact than *dark colored.*

"It was dark colored. Dark green," she insisted.

"Then why didn't you tell the authorities that?" I repeated. "Could it be that you didn't know what color it was? Could it be that when you saw the defendant's car in the brightly lit police garage and saw that it was dark green, you changed your mind about the suspect's car being dark colored and decided that it was really dark green?"

"No, that's not true. I saw a dark green car that night. I'm sure of it. The car I saw by the Wainsgaards' house and the car I saw in the police garage that night were the same car. I'm sure of it."

"You're certainly getting sure. How do you know that it wasn't another Mustang that you saw in front of the home that night? Can you really be sure that it was exactly the same one?"

"I'm absolutely sure," she replied.

"But how do you know? Was there something special about that car? Do you have an exceptional memory?"

"I have a very good memory. I looked that car over really carefully. Like I said, I had never seen a dark green Mustang in front of the Wainsgaards' house before, so I was suspicious. I really took a long, hard look all over that car."

I put my hand out and leaned on the railing. My gut-ache was increasing, but I continued.

"You have a very good memory. You were suspicious, and you looked that car over really carefully. If you were so suspicious, why didn't you check on the Wainsgaards right away? Why did you go over to your neighbor's for twenty or thirty minutes? You must not have been too suspicious," I concluded. I took a few steps back and sat on top of the defense table.

"Now, let's go over this very carefully. You were suspicious, you looked the car over really well, memorizing in your mind every feature, and you have a very good memory. Your memory of every detail of that car is so certain that you are absolutely sure that the car you saw in front of the Wainsgaards' and the car you saw in the police garage are the same. Absolutely sure. Tell me, Mrs. Shears, while you were motivated by your suspicion to look over the car so closely to catch every detail, if it was the same car that you saw later, *then why didn't you notice that it had Arizona license plates?*"

She didn't reply.

"You know, there were probably lots of dark-colored Mustangs on US-89 that night. But there probably weren't very many dark green Mustangs that night on the highway. And there were probably even fewer dark green Mustangs from Arizona. The police would have been gratified that night to have an exact description of the car. But you didn't give it to them. Why not?"

She was quiet for a moment. "It was dark that night," she finally said. "I didn't see the license plates."

"Oh? Didn't you tell us a few minutes ago that it was bright?"

"It wasn't very bright."

"My memory isn't as tremendous as yours, but I think I remember you saying something different. What were her exact words?" I asked the court reporter.

He looked for a moment, then replied mechanically, "'The moon was almost full. And there was snow on the ground, so it was really bright.'"

"Thank you. 'Really bright,' you said earlier. 'Not very bright,' you just said. Which was it? If it was 'really bright,' enough for you to notice the color of the car, why wasn't it 'really bright' enough for you to notice that the license plates weren't from Utah, if it really were the defendant's car? Utah plates have white backgrounds with dark letters, and these were just the opposite, dark background with white letters. Not to mention a cute little cactus and 'Arizona, Grand Canyon State' glaring out in white letters. White is a much brighter color than dark green and would show up in the dark even better. License plates are designed to be visible. Dark green cars are not particularly designed to be visible, especially in the dark. You noticed every detail of that car, except the most glaring, the most important, and the most visible one, if what you're telling us is true, about you being 'absolutely sure' that the defendant's car in the garage and the car you saw on the street that night were definitely the same."

I stood up and approached the witness. "Let's be honest, Mrs. Shears," I said, my voice getting soft and friendly. "Isn't it the truth that you just casually looked at the car, and all you really saw that night was a dark-colored Mustang, like you told the police and the sheriff, and the rest of your details were made up after you had seen the defendant's car, to bolster your story? You didn't lie. But didn't you exaggerate a little, adding just a little to the story, and adding a little bit more to it on the stand today? It's human nature to want to improve on a story. Lots of people do it, even honest people. Isn't that what really happened?" I asked gently.

"Bishop Lindsey, " she said, her voice charged with anger and indignation, "I have a temple recommend. I have never lied in my life. I am not lying now."

I started into her again, until Kurt objected that I was badgering the witness. It was true. I was furious, though I hid it well. Judge Hastings sustained the objection, and I said, "No further questions." Kurt had no redirect, so she sat down.

"Listen," I whispered to Hersh, "I need to go for a while. Take over here, OK? He's just got one more witness, and you might not even have to cross-ex. If he tries to show that slide program of his to the jury, object like all get-out, and if the judge lets it in anyway, take an exception."

"I'm no idiot," he replied.

I strode from the courtroom, quickly ran downstairs to the vending machines, and put in two quarters. I pushed a button, but nothing happened. I pulled down the coin-return lever, and again nothing happened. I pushed the button again without success. I shook the machine, but still nothing came out. I shook it more violently. Finally, I slammed the glass viciously with the flat of my palm. The glass cracked and cut my hand. Though the cut wasn't deep, it was long, and blood started oozing from the cut. I didn't want to drip blood on the floor, so I put my hand in my pocket. I got out forty cents in exact change and put that in the machine. I pushed the button, and a tiny half-pint carton of milk came out.

I seized it, rushed to the agricultural agent's office, and sat down. I opened the first fold on the carton easily, but with just one hand I couldn't open the second fold. The door opened behind me, and I heard someone come in, but I didn't look up. Using both hands, while dripping blood on the carton and the desk, I tried to pull the second fold open, but my hands were shaking so badly I couldn't do it. With a cry of fury, I threw the carton at the wastebasket. It hit the wall behind the wastebasket, but the carton ricocheted in, knocking the wastebasket over.

"You're bleeding," Lisa said, looking at my cut hand.

"I'm OK," I said roughly. I took my handkerchief out and wrapped my hand up. I tried to tie two corners of the handkerchief together to hold it in place, but I couldn't do it with one hand.

"Let me help," Lisa said, reaching for the handkerchief.

I jerked back and finally managed to tie the handkerchief on by using one hand and my teeth. I watched the red line on the handkerchief slowly swell in size. I applied direct pressure for a few moments, then let go. The red area didn't get any larger.

Lisa got up and walked over to the wastebasket. She reached down to pick it up, but I said, "Please don't. I'll take care of it."

She looked at me curiously.

"I prefer to clean up my own messes," I explained.

She walked out of the room. A moment later she was back with a carton of milk, which she opened and handed to me. I gulped it down.

In spite of my rudeness to her, there were pity and deep concern in her eyes. I got up and righted the wastebasket, picking up the papers and trash that had spilled.

"It's not my job to deceive or distort. It *is* my job to test the competency and veracity of the prosecution's witnesses. One of them is incompetent, and the other one is a liar," I said bitterly.

"I gave that woman every chance to tell the truth. I showed her that we knew she was lying, then I backed up and tried to let her off easy by suggesting that maybe it was only a little mistake. But she dug her own grave. Her testimony was the last slim chance that truth and justice had! Why do people have to do that? Why do they try to improve the truth? Why couldn't she just say, 'It was a dark-colored Mustang,' and let it go at that? Now I've got to go back and rub her nose in it! I've got to prove that she's a liar! Kurt didn't have much to go on before, and now because of her he's got nothing! Nothing!" I slammed my fist on the table—the red blotch again started to grow, and I had to apply pressure on the wound once more. "You heard her. Temple recommend and all. 'Never lied in my life.'"

Lisa had sat quietly throughout the entire outburst. "Maybe she doesn't remember that she's lying," she said softly. "Maybe she lied when she saw the car in the police garage in order to 'help' the police, a lie for a good cause. But the lie grew so much that now it's the truth for her. I mean, maybe now in her mind she really remembers a dark green car because she's told herself so often that it was dark green."

"But people, good people, shouldn't be that way," I insisted. "I remember when Johnny Joseph was born. Carol took him down to Las Vegas to visit her family for a few weeks like she always does when she has a baby. One day Johnny got sick—high fever, diarrhea, really listless—so Carol took him to the doctor. Before she left, Carol's little brother, Jason, asked Carol why the baby was a little bit blue. Carol told him that Johnny probably wasn't getting enough oxygen. So when Carol's youngest sister came home, Jason told Margie that the baby was having trouble breathing and had turned blue. He just added a little to the story. Margie told Vanessa when she came home that Johnny was gasping for breath. Vanessa called me up and said that Johnny had stopped breathing. I got all scared and got ready to take off for Las Vegas. Before I went, I called Brother MacDonald and told him that Johnny had stopped breathing, then asked him to tell the kids when they got home from school.

I called Mom in Salt Lake and told her about Johnny having stopped breathing. Mom called all the relatives and told them that Johnny was dead, and Brother MacDonald told his wife the same thing. Before I got out of the driveway, half of the Relief Society was at my house, sobbing. In the middle of all that, Carol called me—Johnny had just had a stomach virus.

"Those were all good people who wouldn't think of ever deliberately telling a lie. But they all expanded the truth. Each one made Johnny a little bit sicker, until Mom and Brother MacDonald finished him off."

I was silent for a moment. "Like Aunt Harriet. A great amateur historian. In her younger days she grabbed up all the information she could about the Lindseys, put it all together and made a great family history. She told nothing but the truth, no matter how it might make the family look. But as she got older, she changed. She put down only the things that made us look good, and eventually she started making up things. Like my Vietnam experiences. I wrote them down for her exactly as they happened, but I guess they weren't exciting enough for her. When I read what she'd put down in the family history, I was amazed at what a hero I'd become. Heck, I'm no hero. Never have been. I'm just an ordinary guy who's always done what needs to be done, no matter how scared I might be."

"Isn't that all that a hero really is?" Lisa asked, smiling gently.

The tension ebbed from me. I smiled too, a little embarrassed at the praise. "'The Lord God hath given you the tongue of the learned, that you should know how to speak a word in season to him that is weary,'" I quoted. "Thank you, Lisa. I needed that. Between you and Carol, I might just come through this with a little of my sanity."

Hersh burst into the room. "Hey, the prosecution's rested its case. Vanderhoft called the sheriff to the stand, and then he tried to show all those gory slides of the murders. But I objected, and the judge sustained it. So the sheriff didn't have much to say, just the bare facts of the murder. On cross-ex I managed to establish the facts that no murder weapon was found on our clients and that they had conducted an intensive search between the scene of the murders and the Cannests' front yard. Sheriff Stronberg did us more good than harm. Things are looking just great!" He rubbed his hands together happily.

"After the prosecution rested, did you move for a dismissal?"

"Sure I did. I know what I'm doing. But the judge said no. You did a great job, John. But you should have come down harder on that retard. Just ripped her apart."

"We made our point," I replied. "No sense beating on the poor thing. She's a good girl."

"Yeah, I guess. Hey, Bryan's folks are here, and they've invited us out to lunch. Any good places in Manti?"

"Ohana's good. Just up the street. Oriental food."

He grimaced. "Well, what if they don't like Oriental? I mean, they're pretty high-class, but they're Chicano. Any good Mexican food around here?"

"The Ohana's good," I repeated. "They have a varied menu, if they don't like Oriental. Or there's a hamburger joint down the street."

"Well, I guess we can find out what they like. Let's go."

I shook my head. "You go. I'm staying here. I don't feel too great at the moment."

Hersh's eyes roamed appreciatively over Lisa's face and figure. "You want to come? Glad to have you," he offered.

She smiled and shooked her head. "No thanks."

He arched his eyebrows, then gave me a knowing wink.

"You want I should lock the door for you?"

"You want I should punch your lights out for you?" I replied. "She's my beloved cousin."

"Oh. Sorry." He left and shut the door behind him.

Lisa laughed merrily. "A knight in shining armor, defending my honor."

"He was out of line."

"He's from a different culture," she said. "L.A. has its own rules."

"L.A. has plenty of good people," I replied. "Hersh is a jerk in any culture. Hersh should have gotten immunity for Bryan and helped put Montague away. He just doesn't give a hoot. He's getting his bucks."

"Unfortunately, there aren't too many John Lindseys in the world," she observed.

"Flattery will get you everywhere," I said. "You want to go down the street with me and get a hot dog?"

"Sounds elegant," she smiled. "I turned down an Oriental dinner for a hot dog. Are you going to slice yours down the middle?"

I laughed for the first time that day.

Chapter Sixteen

After lunch, I dropped Lisa off at the courthouse to assist Professor Fields, then drove home to pick up my camera. Carol reminded me that I had permitted Brenda to take the camera to the Y for her photography class. Carol noticed the bloody handkerchief around my hand, and she fussed over my wound for a while, bandaging it up properly and kissing it better. She then gave me a relaxing back rub to relieve some of my tension. When I finally looked at my watch, I noticed that I was almost late for court. I gave Carol a hurried kiss and rushed back to Manti. As I entered the courthouse, Hersh, who was standing at the door, gestured frantically at me.

"Sorry. Have they already started?" I asked.

He shook his head. "We've got five more minutes. I need to talk to you. My client wants to testify."

My heart leaped for joy! There was justice in this life after all! Bryan's conscience had gotten to him, and he was going to spill the beans! I ecstatically followed Hersh into the agricultural agent's office. He shut the door.

"Have you talked to Kurt yet?" I asked eagerly.

"What about? Bryan wants to testify. He wants to make sure there's an acquittal here, so he's come up with a good, plausible story. Just the icing on the cake, to make sure they go free."

The height of my elation a moment before was countered by the depth of my despair. It took awhile to sink in.

"What're you talking about? Are you suborning perjury?" I asked.

"Look, we're supposed to zealously act in our client's best interest."

"So when are you going to start acting in his best interest? Do you think a few years in prison for perjury is in his best interest?"

"What can they do to him?" he asked. "The exclusionary rule won't let them use the wallet-and-money evidence against him, so they couldn't make a perjury conviction stick."

"What law school did you graduate from?" I asked. "One of those that advertises on the back of matchbooks? The exclusionary rule doesn't apply to his perjury trial afterwards."

He looked at me as if I were telling him something new.

"Listen," I continued, "if you want to put Sanchez on the stand, fine. But the second he utters a single untruth, I'm going to do my duty by stopping the trial and demanding to be excused from the case. That's going to tell the court louder than words that he's committing perjury. Your client does not have the right to lie under oath. And if all this is news to you, you ought to drop out of law and try selling vacuum cleaners. You'd be good at that."

"Hey, let's not get personal," he replied. "We've still got a trial to take care of. Let's not fight each other when we still have a prosecutor to fight."

I left him without a word and went to the courtroom. Though the overhead lights were on, the room was darker than before because thick black paper had been taped over the windows during lunchtime to shut out the light. I sat down by Montague, and Hersh sat by Sanchez. He whispered something in Sanchez's ear.

"Why not?" Sanchez asked. Hersh whispered some more, and Sanchez gave me a dirty look.

It was our turn. We didn't have much to say, but we didn't lie. I first introduced jail records showing that Montague and Sanchez were exactly the same size, to counter Wendy's testimony. Then we called to the stand Dr. Wallace Fields from the University of Utah. Most attorneys don't care for expert witnesses; we don't like to put people on the stand who have great expertise in an area we know little about, because they often say things we don't expect or want them to say. But sometimes we need them, and if we can pay their fees, they're glad to cooperate. The worst thing about expert witnesses is that both sides can usually find experts to support their different points of view, so after the two opposing experts have spoken, the jury becomes even more confused than when it started.

Dr. Fields established his credentials in an impressive manner and went on with his comments. I had learned about night vision while on ambush patrols in Vietnam, and I knew that colors in darkness appear in various shades of blues and black. Dr. Fields told the jury the same thing and explained about cones and rods. Jury service can be educational.

We then turned out the lights and turned on a special light that Dr. Fields said exactly simulated the intensity of the moonlight on the night of the murders. With Lisa's help, he handed out twelve model Mustangs to the jury. They passed the cars among themselves.

Dr. Fields told them that some of the cars were black and some were not. He asked for those who thought they weren't holding a black car to raise their hands. Not one juror raised a hand. Dr. Fields chortled. He asked for the overhead lights to be turned on. Two of the jurors were holding black cars, six were holding dark green cars the same color as Montague's car, and the other four were holding cars painted a number of different dark colors. In simulated moonlight they had all appeared solid black. I showed the jury a photograph of Montague's car to demonstrate that it was the same dark green as the color of six of the models they held.

Our point was proved, but Dr. Fields chose to continue. He was getting a kick out of this. Lisa turned off the overheads and turned on the moonlight, and he passed out another dozen model cars. He asked each person to determine the true color of the car he or she was holding. Then the overheads were turned on again, and Dr. Fields asked the jury if any of them had been correct. Only the lady holding the light blue car raised her hand to indicate that she had guessed correctly.

Dr. Fields then asked Lisa to douse the lights again, but I interrupted him with a smile. "Thank you, Dr. Fields. I think that demonstrates to the jury just how difficult it is to determine colors at night."

He looked at me resentfully for interrupting his fun, but I continued. "Dr. Fields, you heard Mrs. Shears testify today that no cars passed by while she was looking at the suspect's car. There were no street lights in the vicinity, and lights from neighboring houses didn't provide much light. Under the lighting conditions that Mrs. Shears has testified to, if Mrs. Shears had seen the defendant's car parked outside the Wainsgaard house, would she have seen a dark green car?"

"Not a chance. It would have appeared black to her, not dark green."

I thanked him. Having regretfully thrown the last shovelful of dirt on the grave of Mrs. Shears's credibility, I turned Dr. Fields over to Kurt for cross-examination.

Kurt had known that Dr. Fields was coming, but he had been unable to find an expert who was willing to contradict the laws of optics. He declined to cross-examine, and the defense rested.

It wasn't even two o'clock yet. The judge called Kurt, Hersh, and me to the bench to ask us if we thought we could finish our closing statements by four, or if she should adjourn and finish the whole thing tomorrow.

"We can keep it under an hour, easily," I said. "We're ready to go." I didn't want to extend the agony another day.

"I don't know—I'll try to keep it short," Kurt said, as if he had volumes of evidence to review.

As Hersh and I sat down, he asked me if he could give the closing statement. With Sanchez's folks here, he obviously wanted to make it look as if he'd done something to justify his fee. It wasn't always the best strategy to get the jury used to one attorney and then switch to another, but the way things were going, it looked like the only thing that would keep Montague from an acquittal would be if he were to jump up and confess. But with that big smile on his face, he didn't look like he was in a confessing mood. So I told Hersh to go ahead and take it.

He did a really good job (or a really bad job, depending on whether or not you liked to see justice being done). In half an hour he pointed out all the flaws in the prosecution's case, the doubtful credibility of its witnesses, and the total lack of concrete evidence tying the defendants to these murders. He expressed his shock at the brutality of these senseless murders and commiserated with the plight of the poor, blinded orphan. He showed how the prosecution had not only failed to meet its burden of proof, but had senselessly kept two men imprisoned for months in spite of lack of evidence. If you could overlook the smooth deception, it was quite impressive. Hersh finished and sat down, obviously pleased with himself.

Kurt then presented his summation. Though he didn't have much evidence, he kept talking as if he were being paid by the word. At half past four, Kurt finally finished.

The judge proceeded to charge the jury. Judge Hastings emphasized that the prosecution had the duty of proving beyond a reasonable doubt that the defendants were guilty. If any reasonable doubt remained, the defendants should be acquitted.

After the jury was sent out to do its duty, Montague stretched out his legs, put his hands behind his head, and grinned at me. Sanchez wasn't as complacent. He fidgeted in his seat and kept asking Hersh if he really thought they'd be acquitted. Sanchez's father, a big, fine-looking man who was slightly balding, sat down by me.

"Why didn't you let my son testify?" he asked in the same tone of voice that an irate parent would use on a Little League coach for not giving his child enough playing time.

"Ask your son."

"I'm sure he doesn't know."

"Well, Mr. Sanchez, it's not the kind of thing I can discuss."

"Why not?"

"Lawyer-client privilege," I replied.

"Look, because you didn't put my son on the stand and allow him to explain, it makes it look like he has something to hide. People are going to automatically suspect that my son was involved in this murder. The evidence we've seen today proves that my boy didn't have anything to do with this—it was just a case of being in the wrong town at the wrong time. But you've made it look like they were guilty. I'm sure most people figure, 'If he's innocent, why doesn't he testify?' And now you've gone and endangered my son's chances. I know that my son didn't have anything to do with that robbery or murder. My son wouldn't do anything like that. But now you've ruined his reputation and possibly sent him to prison, and I want to know why!"

"Sorry," I said.

"It's lawyers like you that give the profession a bad name," he said icily and walked off.

Lisa was sitting behind me and heard the whole thing. She put her hand on my shoulder and asked me if I wanted her to bring me anything to snack on.

I reached into my pocket and pulled out thirty cents. "How about some Red Hots or some Cinnamon Drops?" I asked.

"Johnny, that's going to be awful on your ulcer."

I turned around and looked at her. "Lisa, I'm getting enough guff from everyone else today. I don't need any from you."

Without a word, she walked briskly away. I immediately regretted my words and my tone of voice—after all, she cared.

I stood up and walked over to the window, poking a hole in the black paper so a gleam of light could shine through. I ripped a whole chunk of paper away and crumpled it up. Reaching through, I opened the window. A sudden gust of wind rattled the remaining paper and mussed my hair. It made me feel better. I walked back to the defense table and sat down.

A box of Red Hots plopped down on my lap, and I looked up. "Thank you, Lisa."

She didn't reply. She sat down in back of me.

"I'm sorry," I said.

She still didn't say anything. I went back and sat down next to her.

"I was rude and out of line. I'm sorry," I repeated.

She was silent for a moment. "So am I," she said softly. "You're taking a beating. It's not fair to expect it not to affect you. You're not Superman."

I shook my head. "I'm afraid that this fight for truth, justice, and the American way is taking its toll on me. I'm beginning to wonder what the American way has to do with truth and justice. I know something's wrong with me when I start being rude to those who're concerned about me. I don't take out my problems on Carol, and from now on I promise not to take them out on you."

"That's OK," she said.

I opened the box of Red Hots and offered her some.

"No thanks. I've never really cared for hot things."

"Neither have I," I admitted, "until the doctor told me to avoid them." But I didn't eat any.

She reached over the chairs and took a legal pad off the defense table. She pulled a pen from her purse and drew up a little tic-tac-toe design. We had played a lot of tic-tac-toe when we were younger. I had usually won then, but I had been so much older than her. Now she beat me six times and we tied eleven times, without a single victory for me.

"You've improved your game in the last twenty years," I observed.

She smiled. "I let you win before. In the early sixties the dumb blond was the rage. A brainy brunette who let a guy know that she was smarter than him didn't get a lot of dates."

"It never bothered me," I answered. "And you never lacked for dates."

"I never let the guys know that I had a brain. Except you. But I still let you beat me at tic-tac-toe and chess."

"You let me beat you at chess? I don't believe it."

"Wait till we get home," she replied. "I'm not as good as Carol, but I'll beat you easily."

It occurred to me that rather than deriding me, she was trying to divert my mind from what was going on in the jury room. I appreciated that.

"Kurt's got a chess set in his office, if you care to prove your statement," I challenged. We went to Kurt's office, where Gwen lent us his chess set. We set the game up in the agricultural agent's office. It didn't take Lisa long to take most of my pieces, and then she appeared to slack off.

"Darn it, Lisa, don't be so patronizing," I protested.

"What are you talking about?" she asked.

"You deliberately moved your bishop right into my queen's field of fire. You don't have to go easy on me."

"My bishop is just fine," she said demurely.

I shrugged my shoulders and took her bishop with my queen. It's no fun when they *let* you win a few.

Lisa brought her knight up and took my queen. "Checkmate," she announced with a slight smile on her lips. I laughed and shook my head.

After we gave back the set to Gwen and re-entered the courtroom, the return of the jury was announced. There was an excited shuffle as everyone settled into his seat. I noticed an artist making a quick sketch of Montague and me.

We arose when the judge entered. Then the jury filed in. Except for a middle-aged lady who looked at me and smiled, they were a sober-looking bunch. The judge asked the defendants to stand. Montague and Sanchez rose, as did Hersh and I.

They were found *not guilty* of all charges.

There was a joyous commotion in the courtroom. Sanchez's father and mother ran to their son and smothered him with hugs. Hersh shook hands all around and accepted a lot of congratulations.

I stood rigid and unmoving, still facing the jury box. I dared not blink, lest the moist warmth that was gathering in my eyes get splashed onto my cheeks.

Chapter Seventeen

"Well, Bishop, you've done me proud," a voice by my side said.

I reached into my pocket and pulled out my bloody hand-kerchief. I pretended to wipe my nose while I got rid of the tell-tale excess moisture in my eyes. I put the handkerchief back into my pocket and turned to face Montague. He had his hand extended out to me. I looked at the hand but didn't move. He put it down.

"No need to be a bad sport, Bishop," he said with a malicious laugh. "Of course, I guess it kind of cuts you up to realize that the things you believe in are a bunch of bull. But hey, don't worry, I can find a place for you in my organization when I get it going. You're resourceful under pressure, and I guess it took a lot of guts to do what you've done, in spite of the way you feel. If you got your head on straight, I'm sure that a hard-working guy like you could be a lot of help to a guy like me. What do you say, Bishop?"

"Can I give you some advice, Montague?" I replied. "It's the last free advice I'll give you, so you'd better listen. The gag order has expired. Pretty soon everyone will know what hap-pened here today and what happened there that night. The people of this valley are law-abiding. But everyone has their limits. If you stay around here, lording it over everybody, by to-morrow morning I wouldn't be too surprised to read that they found your body in an irrigation ditch. Get in your car and ride. You be out of here in five minutes, or I'll file charges against you for that sock on the jaw you gave me."

"My, aren't we the bad sport today?" He grinned.

"Five minutes."

He left.

I sat down in the prosecutor's chair and buried my face in my arms. I felt a hand on my shoulder and looked up into Ed Alvirez's eyes.

"I'm sorry, John, " he murmured.

I sighed. "Ed, tell Sheriff Stronberg that there's a pistol hidden about two-and-a-half miles south of Manti in the old Svenson place. He'd better pick it up before some kids find it and accidently get hurt."

"Thanks, John," Ed replied, and left.

"Bishop Lindsey?"

I turned around. It was the smiling juror.

"Bishop Lindsey, you don't know me, but I'm Helen Olsen's cousin. Agnes Robbins. I just wanted to tell you that I think you did a fine job today."

"The judge asked you at the start whether you knew me or any of the parties, and you said you didn't. She'd have struck you from the jury if you knew me," I said.

"I didn't know you," she said, smiling. "But I remembered Helen telling me about her Bishop Lindsey and what an outstanding guy he is. So when that witness called you Bishop Lindsey, well, it suddenly occurred to me that you must be the one."

"Yes, Helen's my neighbor and a good friend."

"Well, I thought so. And do you know what I told those people in the jury room today when they were trying to decide on a verdict? Some of the jurors wanted a conviction, but I told them about you and what a fine man you are and told them that a decent man like you would never be defending these guys if they were guilty. And it changed their minds, too."

She talked on for a few minutes until I excused myself. I

went back to the judge's office. The light wasn't on. I tried the door anyway, and it opened. The secretary wasn't in, but a light was on in the inner office. I knocked on the door.

"Who is it?" a gruff voice asked.

"John Lindsey."

"Come in," she sighed. Judge Hastings had taken off her judge's robes and was wearing a blue outfit. Her head was buried in her arms, just as mine had been a few minutes earlier. "What do you want?" she asked, not raising her head.

I told her the story that Agnes Robbins had told me. "So if what she says is true, the verdict wasn't based on the evidence at all."

"Oh, John, what does it matter?" she asked, raising her head. She had never called me by my first name before. "If they hadn't acquitted those men, I would have had to arrest the judgment. This case should've never come to trial. Vanderhoft didn't have a stinking chance after I threw out the wallet."

In a move commonly called "judgment notwithstanding the verdict" but referred to as "arrest of judgment" in Utah, a judge has the power to overturn a jury's verdict. It was rarely used, and then only in cases where the judge was certain that the evidence didn't justify the verdict. I thought to inquire why she didn't dismiss the case after the prosecution had rested, but I was too chicken to ask.

"I should have granted that motion to dismiss," she said, answering my unspoken question. "But I'm a coward. I wanted the fault to lie with the jury, not with me. I couldn't take that responsibility. I hoped and prayed that the jury would acquit them because otherwise I'd have had to disregard their verdict and set the accused free. And you know what happened to the last judge in Utah who did that. I don't want my court picketed."

Recently an accused rapist was convicted by a jury. A judge overturned their verdict, saying that there wasn't enough evidence to justify it. The women's leagues were not gentle in showing their displeasure, and they still haven't forgotten.

"John, all my life I've believed in the law. I've worshipped the law. It's not perfect, but I always thought that it was the best system that we imperfect humans could devise. It always tried to achieve justice. My goddess died today, and I helped to kill her."

She put her head back down on the desk. I didn't say anything.

"I've been in here hiding from the predators," she said finally, standing up. "I guess this just about shoots any chances I had at a Supreme Court appointment. I'm a political hot potato now. Well, counselor, let's go out and face the wolves together."

She opened the door for me and we walked down the narrow corridor together, getting closer to the loud clamor in the main hallway. It was obvious that the cat was out of the bag. A reporter rushed up to the judge, followed closely by a host of others. A crew with a Minicam was making their way toward us.

"Ma'am, is it true that the victim's bloody wallet was found on one of the defendants, but you wouldn't allow it to be used as evidence in the trial?"

"Yes. Get out of my way," she ordered.

A microphone was thrust in the judge's face, and bright lights glared in our eyes.

"Why didn't you let them use the bloody wallet as evidence? Was it too gory?"

"Out of my way!" she yelled. She pushed her way through them like a fullback until we got abreast of where Nick Hansen was standing. He was talking to a group of reporters. Though he had had no part in the trial, he was here to get his name in the papers as the local legal commentator.

"Yes, and I'm afraid that as long as attorneys like him are allowed to practice, we will continue to see travesties of justice like we witnessed today," Hansen was saying. "Attorneys like him are far more concerned about winning and getting rich than in achieving justice."

"MR. HANSEN!" The judge's bellow carried like a Marine drill sergeant's yell. "You will follow me to my office! Immediately!"

Hansen's confident face suddenly fell. He meekly followed the judge out.

"How are you feeling, Johnny?" a voice behind me asked. It was Jerry Newcarter. He didn't have a voracious look on his face like the other reporters. He looked human, even concerned. From him, that was surprising.

"Pretty lousy, to tell the truth," I replied.

The Minicam turned on me, and I blinked in the glare. A microphone was thrust in my face.

"Bet it's been tough on you," Jerry continued.

"Hasn't been any picnic," I agreed.

"What happened in there?" he asked. I realized that his kindness may have been calculated to get me talking, but it was OK. At least he wasn't being pushy and rude.

"Our legal system fell on its face," I replied.

Reporters started gathering around, and more mikes were pushed at me.

"Is the law really that rotten and stacked in favor of the criminals?" Jerry asked.

I shook my head. "The law tries to be good and fair. We had a case here where the law got perverted."

"Kind of like the dark side of the Force?" someone asked, and everyone laughed except me.

"Tell me, counselor, " a voice behind me asked, "did you get a nice fat fee for perverting the law and getting a couple of murderers off on a technicality?"

"Hey . . ." Jerry said angrily, and several reporters turned on the newcomer with displeasure. They had cultivated me so well and were about to reap a harvest of information, when this creep had to come along and plow it under. I turned around.

He was a tall kid with a bad complexion and greasy hair. He had a pencil and pad but didn't have anything identifying the paper he represented.

I looked him straight in the eye. I stared at him, and he stared back. He was supposed to lower his gaze when he saw the absolute integrity in my eyes, but he didn't. I turned and walked away.

More microphones were thrust at me, more bright lights glared at me, and more questions assaulted me, but I pushed steadily through the crowd and shoved my way outside.

"Johnny!"

I stopped, and Lisa ran up to me. She took my arm. Normally I might have been disturbed by such an action. But I understood her gesture, and I didn't care if the rest of the county misunderstood. Arm in arm, we walked to my car and drove away.

Chapter Eighteen

Carol stood up when I came through the front door. She was red faced. The TV was on.

"Have we been on TV already?" I asked.

She nodded, staring at me strangely. "Channel Two had a live report," she said shakily. "They said those two were acquitted."

I sat down on the couch.

"They say that one had Brother Coombs's bloody wallet in his pocket when they were arrested," she continued.

I nodded.

"They were guilty," Carol concluded.

I nodded again. "But not legally."

Carol bit her lower lip. She continued to stare at me. Then she walked into the kitchen and stayed there.

I listened to the weatherman apologize for the storm that had failed to show up, in spite of his prediction. I wondered how the people in his ward felt about having a bishop like him who was wrong so much of the time.

Carol still hadn't come out of the kitchen. I figured that the kids had eaten and that dinner was waiting for me in the kitchen, but I chose not to go in. At about seven, Cindy came in.

"Hi, Cindy," I said. She looked at me hatefully and went upstairs. She came down a minute later and went back outside.

Fifteen minutes later, Paul came in. He was carrying a paper sack from 7-Eleven.

"Hi, Dad."

"Hi."

He sat down next to me. "Want some M&M's?"

I shook my head. I don't care much for candy. I'm big on nuts and berries. Paul ate enough chocolate to make a dermatologist's mouth water, but nary a zit appeared on his face.

"They're peanut," he explained.

I looked at Paul. He didn't usually care for M&M's with peanuts. He preferred the pure unadulterated chocolate taste of plain M&M's. I'd never seen him buy peanut before.

"Sure, I'd like some," I said.

He tore the half-pound package open. He kept pouring the little colored ovals until they started spilling over the edges of my cupped hands. "Hey, that's plenty," I said.

We sat together silently, crunching the candy. When I had eaten all of mine, he dumped out another bunch for me.

The front door opened, and Susie came in. "He is not!" she shouted out the front door. She ran past Paul and me. She was crying.

"Hey, Susie, want some M&M's?" Paul asked, but she continued into the kitchen. I could hear Susie sobbing and Carol trying to comfort her.

I turned to Paul. I looked at my third son as he put another handful of candy into his mouth. He was too good to be true. "Your friends been giving you a hard time?" I asked.

He shrugged. "What do they know?"

We continued to eat M&M's until we finished them off.

He brushed his hands off on his pants. "See ya," he said. But with a twinge of guilt, I noticed that instead of going outside to be with his friends, he went upstairs to his bedroom.

A little while later, Carol came in with a tray. "The bishop won't come to his dinner, so the dinner comes to the bishop," she said flatly. She set the tray on the end table, keeping a safe distance from me. After having fulfilled her duty, she went back into the kitchen.

I picked at the food without much appetite. A quarter pound of M&M's will do that to you. After I ate as much as I felt like eating, I took the tray back into the kitchen. Susie's head was on Carol's lap, and Carol was staring out the bay window.

"Thank you," I said.

"You're welcome," she replied emotionlessly, still staring out the window.

I went back into the living room and sat down. I turned the TV on again—there was a Charlie Brown special on.

"Susie, Charlie Brown's on," I called.

"Why don't you go watch Snoopy?" I heard Carol say. Susie came in the living room and sat down next to me. I put my arm around her, and she snuggled up to me as we watched the world's most famous loser.

Lucy was telling us in a commercial to buy Zingers or she'd knock our blocks off, when there was a screeching of tires outside. The Brinkman cars must have gone through a lot of tires since Chris got his license. The front door flew open, and Mark stormed in and confronted me.

"I can't believe you'd do something like that!" he yelled. "You got two murderers off! Just set them free so they could do it again! What's wrong with you, anyway?"

I looked at him for a moment before I answered. "Officer Frost violated their rights, Mark. He pulled them over because of their hair, just like he did to you and Chris and the guys," I said, hoping that Mark's personal experience would generate a little empathy.

"And that's justification for releasing two murderers? What about the rights of the victims?" he shrieked.

Mark was usually so easygoing and lackadaisical that I tended to forget that intelligence tests said he was a latent genius.

Like many other law students, I had memorized sections of Justice Clark's opinion in *Mapp v. Ohio*. I was no longer able to quote it word for word, but I remembered the general idea of it.

"Look, Mark, people always wonder why the criminals go free when the police mess up. It has to do with the integrity of the judicial system. The criminal goes free, if he must, but it is the law that sets him free. Nothing will destroy a government more quickly than its failure to obey its own laws. The policeman is the government's representative. Our government is the teacher, and it teaches by example. If the government becomes a lawbreaker, it breeds contempt for the law, and it invites anarchy. It isn't fair to allow the government to profit by its own illegal acts, and Officer Frost committed an illegal act. He wouldn't have found the evidence if not for the illegal search."

"Then punish Officer Frost! You're sitting there flapping your lips, saying lots of words that sound nice, but it's all wrong. I know it's wrong, and if you don't know it's wrong, then something is wrong with you. Since the law is evil, why didn't you fight the law? You've always said that if one good person will stand up for the right, all the other good people will get behind him, and it's our responsibility to take the lead. But you just let an evil situation run its course without saying a word."

"I was appointed by the court, against my will. I didn't like it, but I'm an attorney," I replied.

"You were talking to Matt once about Brother Cannest, and you said that if a man can't be totally honest and upright in his business, he should change professions. Doesn't that apply to attorneys too, or does it just apply to real-estate guys?"

"Mark," I said tensely, trying to keep from yelling back, "the system isn't bad, it tries to do right. Sometimes it just doesn't work out. I'm not ashamed of my part in it," I said, though that wasn't entirely true. "I was only doing my job."

"Just obeying orders, huh? Just like the SS and the extermination squads. You told yourself so many times that it's right you're now starting to believe it. Somebody else bears the sin, not you. You believe in rigid conformance to the orders of your superiors, right? Too bad you weren't born in Germany. You'd look natural standing on top of a gas chamber with a can of cyanide crystals in your hand."

"Mark!" My voice trembled with suppressed fury. "I've explained my reasons to you. If you can't accept them, that's your problem."

"It's just like Chris says. Everybody has his price. He was

surprised you'd sell out so cheap." Mark turned around and stormed out, slamming the door behind him. I heard tires screech again, and a car roared away.

I was shaking with anger, partly because his arguments sounded better than mine. Susie had watched the whole scene wordlessly. After Mark left, she patted my arm reassuringly. "It's OK, Dad. I think they were innocent."

I exploded, and the anger in me irrationally redirected itself at a new target. "Oh, you do! I hope you've come to that conclusion after meticulously weighing all the relevant evidence!"

Susie's chin started trembling. She got up and ran upstairs, sobbing. I reached forward and clicked off the TV.

Carol stood in the kitchen doorway. "John . . ."

"Yeah," I said, and I followed Susie upstairs. I found her in her room. I tried to take her in my arms, but she pushed me away. "I'm sorry, Susie. I shouldn't have yelled at you."

She kept crying. I took her in my arms again, and this time she didn't resist. She cried in my arms for a while. Finally her sobs subsided, and she just rested in my arms for a long time. "Want to ride our bikes to the Iceburger for an ice cream cone?" I eventually asked.

She nodded. Hand in hand, we went down the stairs and outside. We rolled our bikes from the garage. I had taken the training wheels off her bike only a few weeks previously, so she was still pretty wobbly, but we made it to the Iceburger without mishap. We parked our bikes and walked to the counter. The talk around us ceased for a moment, then continued in whispers.

"Shirley, could we have two twenty-five-cent vanilla cones, please?"

The girl didn't look at me. She filled two cones and wordlessly handed them to me. I set down two quarters and a few pennies. "Thank you," I said. She didn't reply.

Susie and I sat at an outside table to eat our cones. I cautiously looked around. Everyone was taking furtive looks at me. "Look, he's just sitting there, eating ice cream, like nothing happened," one voice said loudly enough for me to overhear.

"Let's go, Dad," Susie said, though her cone was only half gone.

"You'll probably drop your cone on the way back," I cautioned.

"That's OK. Let's go, OK?"

We got on our bikes. I took her cone and held it in my right hand, while I held my own cone in my left. I tried to steer with my wrists. Halfway home, I dropped my cone. I stopped, cleaned up the mess, and dropped it all into Brother Evans's garbage can, hoping he wouldn't mind. We continued home, and I safely delivered Susie's cone to her. She took the ice cream cone and went into the house while I stayed on the front step and watched the sun go down.

When the darkness was complete, Cindy came home. She didn't speak to me as she passed me on the porch. I waited, but Mark didn't show up. I went into the kitchen, and asked Carol if I could help her with anything.

"No, thank you," she responded. She didn't often turn down my offers of help. I left the kitchen.

The Channel Five news came on at ten, and I watched the pretty lights gather together. We were the lead story, and Carol left her self-imposed exile to watch. The reporter told a somber tale.

They showed shots of Montague, Sanchez and his parents, and Kurt Vanderhoft. At the end, there was a five-second clip of me saying, "Our legal system fell on its face."

The anchorman commented, "And that is an accurate summation of today's trial."

I went upstairs to my bedroom.

At a quarter after eleven, I had about decided to turn off the light and go to sleep. Carol had been in our bathroom for a long time. It had been an old trick of hers during those years of law school after my return from Vietnam.

Whatever changes had taken place inside of me in Vietnam, when I came home I was still respectful and loving in my treatment of Carol and good to the kids. I have few solid virtues, but I have always been a good husband. I had not understood the changes that had taken place in Carol during our separation. She had not been mortared, rocketed, captured, or shot, so I felt she had no reason to change. I had spent nearly two years without Carol in Okinawa and Vietnam, but instead of returning to the warm, loving woman that I had left, I came home to a woman who treated me with polite detachment. And there were other more subtle but equally bewildering changes.

Carol would spend long hours during the day reading stories to the kids, saving the dishes, washing, and other assorted chores for bedtime. She was successful in her scheme of coming to bed so late that I was usually asleep. When I finally complained, she retorted that if she got a little more help around the home, she might not be so worn out by bedtime. Although I was already helping as much as my schedule allowed, I naively believed her. I went directly from law school to work, putting on aluminum siding until nine-thirty at night, even during snowstorms and rainstorms. I'd get home at a quarter to ten, hurriedly gobble up whatever the kids hadn't eaten, and then do dishes, fold clothes, and wash out dirty diapers. Carol appreciated it, and showed her appreciation by staying in the bathroom, reading, until I fell asleep. After a while, I caught on. I was no longer a high-priority item on her list. I was the meal ticket for her and the children and the performer of heavy chores.

I suggested marriage counseling, but she said that I was the Vietnam vet, I was the one who needed the counseling. She had already read all that stuff anyway, and she pronounced herself perfectly normal. I went alone for counseling for a while, until the counselor said that it was useless to continue unless my wife showed up too. So she reluctantly came. But she was skillful at diverting the conversation and often led the counselor off on tangents about psychology in general. I was a poor struggling law student and couldn't afford to pay for counseling that merely added to Carol's general knowledge. She could buy psychology books cheaper than that. I decided to get a divorce and told her. She lightheartedly replied that I was too good of a guy to ever leave her and the kids. So I left her. I didn't know what had happened to the happiness I had always felt with her before I went to Asia. I only knew it was gone.

Carol had not realized what a good thing she had going until she lost me. Though poverty drove me back home, I put my bed in the basement until I could get admitted to the bar and make enough money to support separate households.

But I.had a nosy bishop and a pushy stake president, and they both intervened. With new motivation, Carol went alone for counseling, admitting at last that perhaps a problem really *did* exist. She discovered that, in a way, her scars were deeper than mine. I had not considered the effect it could have on a woman to find a grim-faced Marine on her doorstep with a telegram in his hand. When I was missing in action and presumed dead, she couldn't cope with the uncertainty. Emotionally she wrote me off as dead. Even though she later received news that I had escaped from the Viet Cong, it didn't help. Months later, the officer appeared again to inform her that I was critically wounded and struggling for life. She subconciously put on her widow's weeds and recentered her life around her children and her church work. Even when I returned to her more or less whole, she shut me out of her feelings.

Frozen feet don't hurt until they start to thaw, and she had been unwilling to face the pain of thawing. But once she realized that I was serious about leaving her, she became desperate to work out the marriage.

But I wasn't desperate. In fact, I didn't care anymore. I no longer loved her. If Carol didn't value me, I knew that I could easily find someone who would cherish a second-hand but high-quality husband. I wanted out of my marriage as quickly and painlessly as possible. After four years of pain, I no longer trusted her with my heart.

But I stayed. At first, I stayed because of poverty. Then, because it was my duty. Eventually, after a long time, I stayed because I had fallen in love with her again. Some scars remained, and we had lost the innocence that we had enjoyed in our first years together. But she made me happy again, and the thrill that I had felt when I returned home from work each day and found her there had come back. I still bless the memory of a bishop and a stake president who butted in.

As I lay in bed, I knew that if Carol were up to her tricks again, our marriage would not survive. In my youth, after Dad was killed, I had been shut out of my mother's life. Carol had shut me out for over four years. I deserved better treatment than that. I deserved the benefit of a reasonable doubt. I needed her support, if not her understanding. If she shut me out again, it would destroy us.

The bathroom door opened. Carol walked out slowly. She had been crying—her eyes were swollen and red. She blushed a little as she sat on the edge of the bed. I put my hand to her face and stroked her cheek. She bent over and gave me a gentle kiss. And I realized that in their own ways, Lisa, Paul, Susie, and Carol had all told me the same thing.

Chapter Nineteen

Carol had long since gotten up by the time I awoke the next morning. I yawned and stretched, then got up and opened the drapes, letting the sunshine stream in.

"He's up!" I heard Paul yell from outside. I got back into bed and heard footsteps coming up the stairs. My door was flung open, and Brenda came in carrying a big tray.

"When did you get here?" I asked.

"Just this morning," she replied, setting the tray on my lap. I was going to inquire why she was cutting her classes, but I decided that I needn't ask.

Susie set a plate on my tray, and Paul entered with another plate. Johnny came in carrying a salt shaker. "Take it to Daddy," Susie urged, pointing to me. Johnny delightedly sprinkled salt all over the carpeting. I held my arms out to him. He dropped the salt and waddled over to me. I picked him up and set him on the bed. Susie picked up the salt shaker and handed it to me.

Cindy came in with a big pitcher of orange juice and a glass. She slammed the glass on my tray. She sloshed orange juice into the glass and kept pouring even after the orange juice reached the top. The juice spilled over the sides and onto the tray, yet she still kept pouring.

"You little twerp!" Brenda yelled, seizing Cindy by the ear and pulling her from the room. I could hear Brenda whispering furiously to her. Paul came in with a washcloth and started mopping up the spill.

"Thanks Paul, I'll take care of it," I said, but he continued to clean up the orange juice.

"Sorry about that, Dad," he apologized.

"Thank you."

"Here, come on, Squirt, let Dad eat his breakfast," Paul said, picking up Johnny and carrying him out. He shut the door behind him.

It was a great breakfast. There were two eggs fried to leather, two hamburger patties cooked until they were dry and crumbly, and hash browns fried practically black. Brenda was a fine cook—she didn't make any mistakes. She knew the way I liked my food and typically went to special pains to fix it just right. When, as a little kid, I found myself having to cook my own breakfasts, I made lots of errors. But I eventually learned to like and even prefer my mistakes.

After eating, I got dressed in my grubbies and carried my tray downstairs to the kitchen, where Carol was trying to clean a frying pan. I took her in my arms, soapy hands and all, and kissed her. I held her tightly for a long time.

"Thank you," I murmured at last.

"For what?"

I kissed her again and quietly replied, "For loving me anyway."

She colored a little, then kissed me back and told me that Lisa had already gone to the office and that I needn't go in today if I didn't feel like it. So I spent the morning tilling my enormous garden. I went over to the Kanagawa nursery and bought a lot of seeds and plants. When Carol came out to call me in for lunch, she folded her arms and smiled as she looked over my accomplishments.

"Well, Farmer John, what are you planting?"

"Carrots, winter squash, storage cabbage, potatoes, and tomatoes," I replied.

"Carrots and tomatoes are OK, but the kids don't like squash or cabbage. No sense in planting things they won't eat."

"They'll like it when they start getting hungry," I said grimly.

"What about watermelons and cantaloupes? They'll eat lots of those."

I shook my head. "A few, maybe. But they take too much space, and they don't store. I'm not going to put in many this year."

Carol opened a bag. "What's in this sack? Seed potatoes? You always said that potatoes were so cheap that it wasn't worth your time to put them in."

I put my trowel down and looked up at her. "Well, Sweetheart, I'm afraid that my time won't be worth much anymore, so I may as well plant potatoes. I've got enough certified seed potatoes to plant a fifth of an acre."

"A fifth of an acre! We don't eat that many potatoes."

"Well, we're going to have to start."

"John, you talk as if you think the Famine is coming this year."

I nodded. "For us."

"John, that's silly. You're an important member of this community. You don't really think people around here are going to hold anything against you, do you?"

"Carol, two of my own children are holding it against me. Why should I expect the neighbors to be any different?"

"But they're children! They'll get over it."

"Cindy will get over it. She doesn't give a hoot about the moral ramifications of what I've done. She's just sore that I've hurt her social position. If the time comes that she doesn't have to be ashamed of me, then she'll like me again. But Mark is almost eighteen. He's no kid. He confronted me yesterday with questions that I couldn't answer, and he compared me to the *Einsatzkommandos*. He's shaken up. But he's my own son. He knows me pretty well, or ought to. The neighbors don't know me so well—I'm a newcomer by Sanpete County standards. They won't forget, and I doubt if they'll forgive."

"I think you're wrong," she insisted. "These are fine people, just wait and see."

"I will."

She took my dirty hand and we went in for lunch. Brenda

had fixed manicotti, with strawberry shortcake for dessert. Since the rest of the kids weren't there, I was able to pig out to my heart's content. Half an hour later, bloated and satiated, I went back to the garden.

At about five o'clock, Lisa showed up with her kids. "Howdy, Farmer Johnny," she greeted me.

"Are we babysitting again tonight?" I asked, smiling.

"Yes, there's nothing like living close to family members so you can take advantage of their good nature," she replied, then she laughed. "After last week's incident, Leonard said he'd prefer to pick me up and drop me off at my house instead of here."

"Tell Leonard that I guarantee you two won't be bothered again. Cindy got grounded for the weekend, and she knows that next time it'll be for a month." Leonard and Lisa had been on our porch in the middle of a goodnight kiss when Cindy tossed a water balloon from an upstairs window. Fortunately, it missed Lisa. The same could not be said of Leonard's back.

"I guess it's partly my fault," Lisa confessed. "She was obviously inspired by the stories I told your kids about the stunts you used to pull on your sisters' suitors."

"Serves you right for telling tales about me," I replied with a grin. "Where're you and Leonard going tonight?"

"Up to Provo for dinner and a movie," she replied. "Saturday, he's taking me and the children to the Alpine slide."

"Anybody come in today?" I asked.

She shook her head.

"Any calls?"

"Two. Mr. Masters and Mr. Santini called. They both said that they had made other arrangements for their cases and that your services were no longer required."

I rubbed my chin ruefully.

"I'm sorry, Johnny," she said softly. "Sean, why don't you and Jenny go play on the swings," Lisa said to her kids. Jenny obediently ran off to the swing set.

"Johnny, is Susie here?" Sean asked.

"She's in the house."

He went in to find her.

"Susie came home crying today and yesterday," I remarked. "I'm glad that Sean is here for her to play with."

"The principal called me today," Lisa said worriedly. "Sean hit some kids at school. I gave him a good dressing down."

Sean had never been a bully. Like his father, he was big for his age. But unlike his father, he didn't make a habit of slapping people around.

"Why'd he do it?" I inquired, concerned.

"Some boys were bothering Susie at recess," Lisa explained. "Sean went over and told them to leave her alone. Then the boys said something about me, and Sean socked them. One of the boys got a bloody nose."

Though his mother was upset, I was as proud of Sean as if he'd just been awarded the Congressional Medal of Honor.

The Lindseys are not a violent clan. Turning the other cheek is a family characteristic—with one exception. As Sean's antagonist and Jerry Newcarter discovered, when someone bothers a girl under the protection of a Lindsey, they pay through the nose. "Don't be too hard on Sean, Lisa. A guy has the right to defend the girls he cares about, especially his mother. I'm glad he stood up for Susie. It's not her fault that her dad is a jerk."

"Are they giving your other kids a hard time?" Lisa asked.

"Paul's not the kind to complain, but I notice he's been spending the last couple of afternoons in his bedroom instead of with friends. Mark and Cindy have avoided unpopularity by defecting to the enemy. Brenda's been good. Nobody's going to give her trouble at BYU. Even if they did, she'd be on my side. She always enjoys teasing me something awful, but when you get right down to the nitty-gritty, she loves her family as much as she loves herself."

"How did Carol take it?"

I looked at my feet. A big clod of dirt lay there, and I picked it up and crumbled it in my fingers. I looked back at Lisa.

"Pretty hard at first. Until bedtime last night, I honestly

wondered if we were going to make it. It's hard to tell with Carol. I think she'll be OK. At least she's trying. But as brilliant as she is, I still don't think she understands."

"Do you understand, Johnny? I don't—I just accept. I know you too well."

We stood quietly for a moment.

"Lisa!" Brenda called out the back door. "Telephone!"

Lisa and I walked together to the kitchen.

"It's your sweetie pie," Brenda teased, handing the telephone to Lisa. Brenda then picked up a salad and took it into the formal dining room.

"Hello, Leonard!" Lisa said vivaciously, a big smile animating her face. Her smile faded into perplexity. "Why not?" she asked. There was a long pause. "Oh. OK. Goodbye," she said in a quiet voice. She slowly hung the phone up. She sat next to me at the breakfast bar and stared at her hands in her lap.

"What's the matter?"

"Leonard's not coming," she said faintly.

"Why not?"

She didn't answer for a while. "He says maybe our relationship has been moving too fast. He says he thinks we better cool it, not see each other for a while, give ourselves a chance to think things over," she said in a subdued tone, still staring at her lap.

I was flooded with guilt. Susie, Paul, and now Lisa. The sins of the fathers shall be visited on the heads of the children. But on the heads of the first cousins once removed, too? I picked up the salt shaker and squeezed it so hard that my knuckles turned white. "I'm sorry, Lisa. It's all my fault," I muttered.

"No, it isn't," she replied loyally but untruthfully. Her eyes were moist. There was a long silence.

"Would you like to eat dinner with us tonight?" I finally asked, for lack of anything else to say. She nodded. "Brenda," I called, "could you set another place at the table?"

She stuck her head through the doorway. "Sure. Aren't you going out tonight, Lisa?"

"Not tonight," I replied for her.

"How many wontons do you want?" Brenda asked.

"A half dozen will be fine," Lisa said hollowly.

"Is that all? I'm cooking fifty for La Boca Grande here," Brenda said.

Lisa looked puzzled.

"The Great Mouth," I translated. "One of Brenda's affectionate nicknames for her beloved father."

Lisa smiled a little through her tears.

"Better cook up a dozen and a half for her," I told Brenda. "You've never eaten Brenda's deep-fried wontons," I explained to Lisa. "You won't be able to stop at six, Lisa. Nobody has that much self-control."

"You just watch," Lisa replied.

I watched. I watched her eat the six that Brenda had fried for her, and I watched her snitch another dozen from my plate.

The next day at the office during lunchtime, I tempted Lisa with one of Brenda's apple turnovers.

"Johnny, please! I've got to watch my figure," she protested. "I'm still trying to recover from last night."

I took a big bite of the turnover and made delighted noises of pleasure. "There're four more in this sack," I said enticingly. "They're fresh. Brenda just made them this morning." I took another big bite.

Lisa looked at it hungrily, then turned her head away and refused to look at me. "Don't," she said. "I skipped breakfast this morning."

I made another ecstatic groan of enjoyment. "You know," I said, "it's not healthy to gorge and fast."

"It's healthier than gorging and gorging, like you do all the time."

I was about to take another big bite when the phone rang. Lisa answered, then handed it to me. Carol was crying on the other end, and I couldn't understand her. "What?" I asked.

She tried to be coherent. "Johnny swallowed a bottle of aspirin," she wept.

184

"Listen," I said urgently,"give him some ipecac, and I'll be right there. And bring the bottle."

"Are you sure? Is ipecac OK for—"

"Yes, I'm sure," I said and hung up. "Lisa, let me take your car. Johnny swallowed a bottle of aspirin."

A moment later I squealed to a stop in my driveway. Brenda was sobbing on the porch. I was halfway up the sidewalk when Carol came running out the front door carrying a crying toddler. As soon as we had him in the car, Johnny started vomiting from the effects of the ipecac. I rolled down the window as the car filled with the sickening acidic smell. As we flew by Ed Alvirez at twice the speed limit, he turned on his siren and lights and escorted us. He knew that we wouldn't be speeding unless it was an emergency.

I prayed all the way. I couldn't forget a similar mad drive we had made a few years earlier when Johnny Jacob was pronounced dead on arrival. We sped through Manti and Sterling and shortly arrived at the Gunnison Hospital. They checked him while Carol answered their questions and I assured them that I had insurance.

They couldn't find anything. After looking at the empty aspirin bottle, they assured us that he could not have ingested the children's aspirin without leaving any telltale traces of pink blobs. But Carol was certain that the bottle had been full the day before.

The crisis over, I talked a hospital clerk into getting me a bunch of paper towels and a plastic trash bag. I went outside and started cleaning up the mess in Lisa's car. I was trying to clean the floor when I heard someone behind me.

"Mr. Lindsey."

I turned around and saw Roxanne Springhurst, the nurse who had told me about the missing sponge.

"You're quite the hypocrite, aren't you?"

I didn't reply.

"You talked about me being calloused. You told me about a moral duty to help others, and you accused me of not caring about what happened to society. But I never helped murderers get free so they could murder again. I guess lawyers don't owe anything to society, do they?"

I still didn't say anything. I picked up another paper towel and turned back to the mess on the floor.

"Yeah, why don't you wallow in the vomit? It's all you deserve."

I continued to scrub, and she walked away.

Brenda and Carol came out after a little while, carrying a very pale little boy. The doctor said he was fine. We went home.

I continued to clean Lisa's car, trying to remove the odor. Brenda came outside after a while.

"Mom found the aspirin. Sean and Susie were playing nurse yesterday, and they must have gotten the aspirin down. It looks like Johnny took the aspirin from the bottle and put it into Susie's piggy bank."

"I guess a little girl is due for a severe chewing out," I said.

"Dad, why don't you go to work? I can take care of this."

I shook my head. "I finished a court appearance this morning. I don't have any more until next week. I have some things to do, but they can wait. Besides, Johnny's my child. When you have kids, you can clean up after them. But why don't you give Lisa a call? I'm sure she's worried."

"Mom called her from the hospital. You want some lunch?"

"No, I ate a turnover before. And this smell doesn't exactly give me an appetite."

Brenda went back inside, and I eventually got the car as clean as it was going to get. I drove back to the office.

No one came in that day, and I was fired three more times.

That night, someone found a new way to demonstrate his affection for me. A little after midnight, my phone rang. When I answered it, he hung up. Three more times that night, the shy phone caller struck. I wanted to pull the line out of the jack, but since I often received legitimate phone calls at night requesting my services as bishop or lawyer, I restrained myself.

On Saturday, I became convinced of the Postmaster General's wisdom in proposing cancellation of Saturday mail delivery—I received nine letters from clients telling me that my services were no longer required. Then late Saturday night, I finally disengaged my phone after the seventh harassing call.

Sunday morning was the clincher. We had averaged about 62 percent attendance for the year at sacrament meeting. I was glad that Brenda was there to add to our numbers or we would have dipped below 30 percent. I had expected a fall in attendance, but I was surprised at the paucity of worshipers. When sacrament meeting let out, most of the people filed out the west door where my first counselor was shaking hands, even though my door led more directly to the Sunday School classes. A few people endured the handshake of the pariah, but most of them wouldn't look me in the eye. When Sister Kanagawa shook my hand, she looked at me with bewilderment in her face rather than condemnation.

After everyone else had filed out, Tom Kanagawa came up to me. Even he wasn't able to look me in the eye.

"Bishop, can I talk to you after priesthood meeting?"

"Sure." Normally I was pressed by lots of people who wanted to talk to me on Sunday about one problem or another. But since the trial, Tom was the first person to ask for a private interview.

As I walked to my office, I thought about Tom Kanagawa. It occurred to me how ironic it was that during the war, our government had illegally incarcerated tens of thousands of people like Tom even though it knew they were innocent. Now that same government was freeing criminals even though it knew they were guilty. I expected that Tom would ask to be released from his calling as ward clerk.

In my meetings with the ward leaders, I noticed that everyone was uncomfortable in my presence. Nevertheless, we got a lot done. No matter what kind of man their bishop was, they were determined to carry on with their responsibilities.

After priesthood meeting was over, Brother Kanagawa knocked on my door and came in. "Bishop, I don't want to take up too much of your time." He seemed embarrassed, shifting uncomfortably from one foot to another. He looked like he wasn't sure how to say what he'd come to tell me.

"You were right about those blackberries," I said, just to get the talk flowing. "They're coming up all over the place and going crazy. It's really a mess."

"Then you'd better get them trained right away before they really give you trouble," he replied. "Are you still planning to run for county attorney? That's what I wanted to know."

"I guess so. Kurt won't run again, and Brent Crenshaw doesn't want the job. I'm not going to let Nick Hansen run unopposed. I'll know for sure next weekend at the county Republican convention."

He handed me an envelope, then looked at the floor. "Here, take this for your campaign. If the Republicans don't nominate you, keep it for when they do let you run." He raised his eyes and looked me in the face. "If there were several dozen more lawyers like you in California in '42, my mother would never have died of pneumonia in a concentration camp, and my dad wouldn't have died a drunk migrant worker." He turned around and hurriedly limped off.

I opened the envelope. It held a check made out to the John Lindsey Election Committee in the amount of one thousand dollars.

Monday six more rejection letters arrived in the mail, and three more people called Lisa to cancel my services.

Monday afternoon I received a phone call from Mark's English teacher. She wanted to tell him what the reading assignments were so that he wouldn't fall behind while he was sick.

"But Mark isn't sick," I remarked.

"He isn't? But he's missed three of my classes. Last Thursday and Friday, and again this morning. Is he out of town, or what?"

"No, he's been here all along. I didn't know he was missing your class. Has he skipped all his classes?"

"Let me check." A moment later she said, "Yes, he's on the school absentee list."

"Thank you, Mrs. Lysander. I'll check this out."

I hung up the phone. I hadn't seen much of Mark since the night of the trial. He stayed out late at night now and left early in the morning. He came home at odd hours for food. He hadn't shown up at church last Sunday. To my recollection, it was the first time he'd missed church when he wasn't sick.

Normally, I would have rebuked him for the kind of behavior he'd been exhibiting, but I'd been hesitant because my own recent actions had somehow put me in a morally inferior position, and from that position, I didn't feel comfortable in censuring others. But I was his father, and it was my duty to straighten him out.

I found Carol, and told her what Mrs. Lysander had said. "Next time Mark is here, don't let him run out before I can talk to him."

She hesitated a moment before saying, "Do you think maybe it might be better if I talked to him?"

She too recognized my moral inferiority.

"No," I said. "I'll have to talk to him sometime. Might as well be now as later."

Carol looked doubtful but didn't say anything.

I was working in the orchard when Carol called to me from the back door. She said that Mark was home. I went in and found him coming up the stairs from the basement.

"Mark, you've been sluffing school."

"Yeah, so what?"

"Look, you might not think much of your father anymore, and I'm not going to drag a young man who is nearly eighteen to church, but there are laws against truancy."

"So what? If they arrest me, you can get me off on a technicality."

"Mark!" I said furiously, grabbing him by the shoulder. He eyed me coolly. My anger ebbed away, leaving only emptiness. I let go of his shoulder. "Mark, please go back to school," I said quietly, staring at the floor. "If you sluff your last few weeks, you can't graduate. If you really want to hurt me, just don't go to church anymore. Not going to school hurts you more than it hurts me." I turned away and went back outside. There wasn't much else I could say: Mark was sure that I was wrong, and I wasn't sure that I was right.

I went out and surveyed the blackberry patch. I had ruined it. The thorny canes straggled everywhere. They were wrapped around each other, choking each other and blocking each other from the light. I should have gone inside to get some heavy leather gloves, but Mark still might have been in there. I thought about Mark as I got on my knees in the blackberry patch and started to fight to get the plants in order. I thought about Brother Kanagawa's words when he heard what I'd done to my blackberries. Once you've got them, you're stuck with them. They seem to pick up every bad thing that comes along and they don't always have the fruit you expect, but if you handle them right the fruit you get is the best in the world. Yet, if you don't train them right and keep a close eye on them, they'll go wild on you. My unprotected hands became bloodied as I struggled among the thorns to right the mess I'd caused.

After five o'clock, Lisa came by. She admired my garden, then saw my hands. "What have you been doing?"

I looked at my hands with curious detachment. "I dunno. Engaging in a little masochism. Atoning for my sins with my own blood. You and Carol are the shrinks—I'm sure you two will be able to figure me out."

"The patch looks good."

I looked at the reorganized blackberries. "Some of them were too twisted to save. I had to take them out so the others could survive. I got the rest of them supported. I think they'll be OK. Anybody come in today?"

"One."

I looked at her eagerly.

"A guy wanted to know where the post office was. I told him."

My face fell. "And Adney accused me of using this case to drum up business. Any more calls?"

She shook her head. "But at least no one else called to cancel."

"There aren't too many clients left to fire me," I replied.

190

"Johnny, I'm sitting there doing nothing. I've got all the files cleaned out and reorganized. I've got everything in ship-shape, and there's nothing left for me to do. Days crawl by when you're not doing anything. And what's worse, I'm taking your money for nothing."

"Why don't you take a few home-study courses, finish off your degree?"

"But that isn't going to make me feel any better, getting paid to study in your office."

"So are you saying that you want to go back to Richfield?"

She shook her head. "No, that's not what I mean. I just don't want to take your money when I'm not doing anything for it. The answering machine can take care of any calls."

"Well, let's try it till the end of the week. This work has always come in spurts. Feast and famine. No one comes in for days, then a bunch come the same day."

I was kidding myself, and she knew it. I just hated the thought of sending her out to find work after she'd given up a good job in Richfield to help me. If she went back to Richfield, she would probably have to start over again.

"OK," she said, "on Saturday we'll see what we can think of after you get back from the convention."

Saturday morning came, but no clients did. I was putting on my business suit, preparing to go to the convention, when the phone rang. "Hello?" I said.

"Hello, John? This is Abe Tomlinson."

Averal Tomlinson, who preferred to be called "Abe" after that great Republican, was the head of the county Republicans. He and I were good friends, though I was not a solid, rock-hard Republican like him. I would and did vote for Democrats if I thought they were better than their Republican opponents. Abe thought that was base treachery. But he was a good man.

"John, I don't know quite how to put this, so maybe I'd just better spit it out. You'd be better off if you didn't show up at the convention today."

"What do you mean? I'm running for county attorney. And I'm a delegate."

"I just don't want to see you humiliated. Don't show up, OK?"

"Are you going to let Nick Hansen run unopposed? No way, Abe."

"Just let me worry about that, OK?" he said.

"But I'm a delegate. I have an obligation to be there to represent my district."

"You have an alternate to go if you can't make it."

"Sure, but I can make it."

He sighed. "John, I've heard rumors. Some people are planning to . . . show their displeasure. They'll disrupt the convention and demean themselves while they disgrace and humiliate you. It could be ugly, John. I can't order you not to come. But I'm asking you as graciously as I can, please don't come. You won't get the nomination anyway. Please don't let them wreck my convention."

"I'll call my alternate," I said in a subdued voice.

"Thank you, John."

Shortly after he hung up, the phone rang again.

"John, this is Brent Crenshaw. Listen, the Republican committee wants me to run for county attorney. I told them no, I wasn't going to stand in your way. But they've been pressing me. I sure don't want Nick Hansen in there. We've had a clean county so far—Kurt's always been straight. But you know what could happen to the justice system in this county if a guy with Hansen's morals gets the job. He and his friends can really do a lot of damage." He paused as if expecting a reply, but I said nothing.

"I told the committee you had only done your duty, that you had to defend the guy. I told them what a great guy you are. I gave them the whole *Mapp v. Ohio* spiel. But they insist that you're unelectable and that you're going to drag all the other Republicans down with you. I still told them no. They said the whole county is in an uproar. They showed me all the editorials in the local press and the letters to the editors, some even in the *Tribune* and *Herald* and *Deseret News.* But I won't step on your toes. If you hadn't shown me the ropes when I moved to this county and walked me step by step through my first several cases, I would really have been in a mess. I owe you something. If you intend to run, then I'll say no to the committee. But I'll do whatever you say."

I was silent for a moment. "Go for it, Brent," I said finally. "I'm glad that you're willing to take the job. I don't want Hansen in there either. I've read the editorials too and the letters to the editors. None of them mentioned me by name, but I got the message. I guess it was wishful thinking on my part to hope that they were just the extremist crackpots. But if they represent the majority, then you'd better run. In fact, for the sake of the county, I'd say you have no choice. But thanks for sticking up for me, even if it was in a futile cause."

"You won't be sore at me?"

"You're doing us all a favor, Brent."

He thanked me and hung up.

I looked in the phone book for another number and dialed it. "Mrs. Duralsky? This is John Lindsey. Are you too busy today to go to the convention for me? You're my alternate, and you're welcome to go if you'd like."

"Well, sure, I'd like that," she admitted. She had wanted to be the elected delegate, but she had been a distant second to me in the number of votes received.

"OK, thanks. I've got a bunch of papers here that the committee sent me. Come over and get them anytime. The convention is at ten."

After she had thanked me and hung up, I took off my suit and put on my Levis and Star Wars T-shirt. I went downstairs.

"Are you going to the convention dressed like that?" Carol asked.

I shook my head. "No, I'm going to grab a fair maiden and carry her away," I replied. I easily picked her up in my arms and carried her outside. I set her carefully on the bench underneath one of our walnut trees.

"John, I'm busy," she protested.

"We need to talk," I replied.

"What about?"

"Let's move."

"What?"

"Let's move," I repeated.

"John, when you planted these walnut trees, you said that we would still be here to harvest the walnuts. We haven't harvested any yet."

"That is certainly a valid argument for not moving," I agreed. "I'm out of work, I have no prospects, my world is caving in, and we have no walnuts. But unfortunately, wife of my life, we cannot live forever on walnuts, even if we had some. Fortunately, we paid off the house in those days when I was doing well, but raising a family is expensive. We have money put away, but it won't carry us through the winter. And I'm not going to kill myself so you can collect my life insurance. All that money would be worthless to you without me. Right?"

"Well . . ." she began teasingly.

"Of course right." I leaned back against the trunk. "Sweetheart, my profession depends on the goodwill of the community. I have lost the goodwill of all the decent people in this valley, and there aren't enough indecent people to keep me going. I might not be part of President Reagan's official statistics, but for all intents and purposes I am unemployed. Fortunately, I have many building skills and a general contractor's license. Unfortunately, the construction industry is severely depressed. In this county, I could never find a construction job, even if one were available. I can't build homes on speculation either because there's no market for spec homes in this valley, so I'd never get financing. We could sell off a few kids, but you wouldn't like that. So let's move. Back to Salt Lake, or maybe to Provo. Get a new start. It'll be tough for a while starting over at the bottom, trying to get new clientele, but it won't be as tough as staying here."

"What are you going to do in Salt Lake? Practice criminal law?"

"No way. I admire those who can handle it, and someone

has to do it, but I can't. I guess I could build on my reputation now, become a big criminal lawyer and point to the Montague case as proof of my slyness. But it's a rep I don't deserve. I'm a good attorney, but any careful second-year law student could have gotten Montague off. I've had my fill of criminal law. If I can't get any clients, I can always build homes. But we've got to get out of here before we dry up and blow away."

"John, you're overreacting. Things will calm down. People know what kind of fellow you are. Just stay here, and things will eventually pick up again."

"No insult intended, but that sounds like the old line from *Mein Kampf*," I replied. "'The masses have short memories.' But the people here have great memories. They can bore you to tears with the forgotten, trivial exploits of their ancestors back six or seven generations."

"John, don't get bitter against the people around here. You've always said what good people they are."

"They are good people. I bear no animosity toward them, except for the people who've told their kids not to play with Susie. She can't help it if her dad's a bum. I've always liked these people, and I have to admit that their reaction to my crime has been remarkably temperate. No lynch mobs have gathered to get me, I haven't been stoned, no swastikas have been burned into my lawn, and no bricks have been thrown through my window. I haven't been hung in effigy, and no petitions have been circulated against me. So far, only two people have insulted me to my face. The rest of the people are showing their displeasure with the most civilized of weapons, the boycott. Considering the seriousness of my offense in their eyes, I'd say that the folks around here are showing admirable restraint. I understand these people a lot more than they understand me. They have a right to be upset. Three of their neighbors were shot, and nothing happened to the murderer. They forked out money for a trial that mocked justice. An injustice was done here, and they are incensed. Since the defendants are gone, I'm the only target left for them to shoot at. I'm guilty by association.

"These people are a lot better educated than most rural people, but they aren't lawyers. I don't like what they're doing to me, but I understand them, and I don't hate them for it. If there is any bitterness in me, it's toward my own profession. In law school, they told us that in a situation like this, the local bar had the responsibility to come to my defense. They're supposed to write letters to the editors and guest editorials and tell everybody what a swell fellow I am, even though I did get a murderer off. Sure, Brent called today and said that he told the Republicans what a nice guy I am, but he waited until he was asked. The bar is supposed to thrust itself forward and bear the heat with me. But Hansen is sitting back taking potshots at me, Kurt is keeping quiet for fear of hurting his chances at attorney general, and the judge doesn't want to further jeopardize her chance at the Supreme Court. So I'm facing the heat myself. But I can't take it, so I'm leaving."

"It's not like my husband to run when the going gets tough."

"Don't bait me, honey. I know you want to stay here. I don't mind the fact that the going is tough. It's just that I don't see any prospect of it improving. And it's tough on the kids." I looked at her questioningly. "Aren't people giving you trouble too?"

"Our culture expects a wife to stand by her husband," she said matter-of-factly. "To them, I'm the loyal but suffering spouse. However, their clemency doesn't seem to extend to children or cousins. And to be frank, I think it would be a lot worse if you weren't the bishop."

That was probably true, I decided. They respected the office, no matter what they thought of the man who held that office.

"But after a while, things will turn around," she insisted. "Besides, this is a lousy market to try to sell our house. Especially if people know we have to sell. We won't get anywhere near what this house is worth."

"As long as we have money in the bank, we don't *have* to sell. But if we wait until the money's gone before we move, then someone, probably Adney Cannest, will take the house for a song and resell it for a bundle."

"I could put in for substitute teaching," Carol suggested.

Carol occasionally substituted during epidemics of flu and other diseases that kept several teachers home. They had been impressed with her (naturally) and wanted her as a regular substitute, but she had refused.

"Even if the district doesn't hold against you the fact that you're married to such a loser, you couldn't make enough to support the family. And I'm not going to sit around. I'm leaving. I would be gratified if you would go with me. In fact, I'll be crushed if you don't. But I am going."

Carol brightened. "What about county attorney? That's a steady income. And surely the people in this valley would choose you over Hansen."

"Abe just called. I've been asked not to show. Brent is going to run. Anything rather than letting Hansen have it."

"John, can't we just stay here for a while and see how things turn out? Something will change. I know it. God won't let you fail."

"God helps those who help themselves. What makes you think that things will change?"

"My female intuition."

"Well, Carol, I believe in visions, the ministering of angels, direct revelation, inspiration, and the whisperings of the Holy Ghost. But I don't believe in female intuition. For four years my mother told me that her female intuition said that Dad was coming back. But the Japanese admiral who executed Dad didn't believe in Mom's female intuition either.

"God permits good men to be defeated, at least in a temporal sense. I can never be defeated spiritually unless I choose to be defeated. But I have the temporal means to leave and make a new life for myself before I get defeated here. And I'm going to do it."

"Let's stay for a while, John."

"Define *a while*."

"I don't know. A month, maybe longer. But let's stay for a while, OK?"

"Darling, if I could see any sense in it, I'd say yes. But you can't give me a single good reason for it."

"What about your church calling, John? You haven't been released yet."

"I've served for more than five-and-a-half years. They don't usually ask a bishop to serve longer nowadays."

"They used to serve for twenty, thirty years, even for life. It's a calling of indefinite duration—until you're released. I don't recall you saying when you were called that you would serve only for five years."

I sighed. "Carol, I'm being manipulated again. But I'm getting smarter. It used to be that I didn't even realize when you were manipulating me. Now I'm smart enough to recognize it, but unfortunately I'm not smart enough to resist it. Especially when you're right. I'll stay until the Lord sees fit to release me."

Carol was quiet for a moment.

"John?"

"Yes?"

"Did you ever ask the Lord if you were doing the right thing in defending Montague?"

I stroked her hair quietly for a while before answering.

"I spent a good part of an afternoon at the family knoll, seeking guidance, but it didn't come. I was left to go on my own. When I weighed the factors to make up my mind, I wasn't aware that Wendy was blind, leaving the prosecution with no eyewitness, so I blindly blundered ahead. Even in my later prayers, I received no specific answers.

"I didn't have any scriptural precedents to rely on, and there were only a few passages that were even tangentially relevant. 'We believe in being subject to kings, presidents, rulers, and magistrates, in obeying, honoring, and sustaining the law.' 'Let no man break the laws of the land, for he that keepeth the laws of God hath no need to break the laws of the land. Wherefore, be subject to the powers that be, until he reigns whose right it is to reign.' Then there is the story of the people of Ammon. Those converted Lamanites took an oath to never shed blood again and allowed themselves to be killed rather than break their oath. But later, when the Lamanites were about to overrun the Nephites, lots of the Ammonites wanted to take up the sword to help the Nephites until Helaman told them he was afraid that if they broke their oath, they would lose their souls.

"I also took an oath. When I was admitted to the bar, I swore to obey the law of the land. But when it came to this case, I tried to get the Lord to tell me to break the law. But the Lord was silent.

"It's so easy to choose between right and wrong. But I didn't have the luxury of such an easy choice here. I had to choose between several wrongs. Do I violate my oath, break the law by keeping my mouth shut about the illegal search, and let a murderer get what he deserves? Or do I obey the oath I have taken and free a murderer? Or do I irresponsibly neglect my duty by quitting a difficult case, and possibly suffer disbarment? If I'd broken my oath and the state had found out, the state would not have permitted me to continue practicing law. By keeping my oath and setting Montague free, the people have prevented me from practicing in their midst. I've grown to love my profession. It's purposeful—it actively supports the country and its laws, and it aids society. But I could still live with myself even if I couldn't practice law. I'm not sure if I could live with myself if I had walked away from my duty or had violated my own integrity by breaking my oath.

"I almost broke my oath one afternoon by letting the authorities know the location of the murder weapon. But Sanchez would never have told me where the gun was hidden if he hadn't had faith in my promise to keep it confidential. If I had dropped that envelope in that mailbox, my honor and integrity would have gone with it."

I was silent for a moment, then continued. "When the Lord called me to be the bishop, I wondered at his judgment, but I never doubted the fact that he did call me, even though I couldn't figure out why. But I am the bishop, and he has never withheld answers from me about how to fulfill my stewardship and direct this ward. In my daily life, I've been able to lean on him for answers. But on that hill, for once in my life, I was left answerless.

"When I was a child, I thought as a child. Everything was black or white. But now I see through a glass, darkly, and almost everything is in various shades of gray. The only pure white absolutes left in my life are the Lord and his gospel. But even though I've prayed and struggled, I honestly no longer know where I stand with him."

Suddenly, my throat constricted, and my body was shaken with a suppressed sob. I steeled myself against another and silently fought for control. Carol took a corner of her sleeve and wiped away a tear that had betrayed me. She snuggled up to me and looked at me while I stared at the leaves. The spasm passed, and I relaxed. Carol kissed me gently on the cheek. In the house Johnny woke up from his nap and yelled for all he was worth. Carol kissed me again, got up, and left me alone. I continued to stare.

Chapter Twenty

Sunday morning, 39 percent of the ward members were present at sacrament meeting. It was better than the week before but still far short of the yearly average. My first counselor frankly told me that some people were saying that they weren't going to go to church again as long as I was bishop.

Mark was not among those present, but after a few discreet phone calls, I was somewhat comforted to find out that he'd gone back to school. He still wasn't talking to me.

Sunday evening an event of historic proportions occurred in Ammon. There was a burglary. The home of Brother and Sister Eyre was hit. Sister Eyre was the Young Women's president, and she, her husband, and their three daughters were all at the youth fireside when the burglary occurred. Only thirty-five dollars was taken from the house, but fifteen hundred dollars worth of damage was done to mirrors, a grandfather clock, and other personal property. Ammon had never had a burglary before.

Friday afternoon I was in the garden spraying insecticide at anything that moved when Carol and Lisa walked up. "Closing up early today?" I asked Lisa.

"Lisa's quitting," Carol said.

"Just for a while." Lisa added quickly. "I'll come back when you need me."

I turned the sprayer off and set it down. "You moving?"

"Not while I'm getting free rent. Carly at Foodtown had her baby prematurely this morning. Chuck knew I was assistant manager in Richfield. He asked me if I could fill in for a while. School will be out pretty soon, so if he has to he can move a checker up, retrain her, and hire a high-school kid as checker. But he says if I work out he'll keep me as assistant manager if I want. Carly's saying that she would like to stay home and raise the baby. But at any rate, he has to have somebody who knows what she's doing until school lets out. After that he's flexible. It's only for a little while, if I want."

"How much is he offering?"

She told me.

"But you make nearly double that working for me."

"No, I don't. I'm not working for you, I'm just taking your money. Carol told me what you're making, and I feel guilty for taking so much. Chuck says that he'll give me a big raise in several months if I work out. He knows that my first loyalty is to you. But he knows, just like everyone else, that we don't have any work at our office."

"He told her that he doesn't want to see her dry up and blow away like you're going to do," Carol added.

"Johnny, when you need me, you know I'll be right back. And if you have to move, I can stay here until you get established and can afford to hire me again. But I'm not going to take your money when I'm not doing anything for it."

I folded my arms and stared at the ground. I keenly felt my failure and my guilt. I had ruined the social lives of my children and Lisa, and now Lisa had to go to work at bare subsistence wages because she had left her job to help me out.

"I think it's the only sensible thing to do, John," Carol said.

"Moving is the only thing that makes sense," I replied.

"Johnny . . . "

I sighed. "I agree, Lisa. It's the best thing," I conceded.

"You won't be sore?" Lisa asked.

I shook my head.

"You sure?" Lisa asked.

I managed a smile. "Sure. And if Chuck needs another bag-ger, tell him I'm available."

The problem with Mark had also continued. He was at-tending school but wasn't going to church. At home, he was moody and irritable. One night he teased Susie to tears. Carol had a long talk with him. After that, he quit tormenting his brothers and sisters, but he was still touchy and cranky.

Three days later Judge Hastings called me and assigned me to a legal aid case. A woman complained that a neighbor's dog kept getting into her chicken coup and had killed most of the chickens. The rest had stopped laying. The neighbor refused to tie his dog up. We sent the sheriff and dogcatcher after the dog, and I talked the neighbor into compensating the woman for her dead chickens. If I could pick up fifty cases like that a day, I'd make big bucks.

Thursday after midnight, my sleep was interrupted by a phone call. The late-night phone harassment had stopped after a while because a person had to interrupt his own sleep in order to interrupt mine. This phone call was legitimate.

"John, this is Ed Alvirez. I've got a DUI here in jail. He says he's heard all about you and wants you to get him off. I have a couple of his buddies locked up too. I don't know if it's worth coming here tonight. He's still conscious, but he looks like he'll keel over any minute. He keeps saying he wants the same lawyer who got the murderers off. I guess he means you," he said, but a note of apology was evident in his voice.

"I can use all the work I can get," I replied. "I'll be right there."

I dressed quickly, but not quickly enough. By the time I got to the police station, the drunk-driving suspect was lying on the floor of the jail cell with his buddies, sound asleep.

"What happened, Ed?"

"These three were driving on the grass in the park—stoned out of their minds. Some people saw them and com-plained, and I arrested them. Two of the guys were hanging out of the car windows, shaking up cans of beer and pulling the tabs to let the beer fly all over. Then they'd yell, 'It's a gusher!' and laugh like crazy. They did that over and over. I found fourteen empty sixpacks in the car. Brother Cannest—he's one of the ones who complained—says he knows one of the guys. Says he works on the oil rigs outside of Fairview. I guess we'll find out more in the morning."

"I guess so."

Ed looked at me quietly for a moment. "John, I don't know if you knew, but Helen Olsen had a cousin on the jury in the Montague case. Agnes Robbins. She blames herself for the fact that those guys went free since she thinks she talked the jury into an acquittal. She became almost suicidally depressed. Fortunately, her Relief Society visiting teachers noticed and told the bishop before she could do anything stupid, and she's getting professional counseling now. I hear some other jurors are blaming themselves for what happened. Sister Cannest and Bobby Cannest have both come to me because they don't dare talk to you. They both feel that the whole thing is their fault. And Heber has been moping ever since the trial. He feels like it's all his fault, too. He testified at the pretrial hearing, just like Sister Cannest and Bobby, and they all blame themselves. That case, *Mapp v. Ohio*, is in one of our training booklets, and I got it for Heber to try to make him feel better. But he says it's all a bunch of bull. After seeing what it does, I have to agree with him. And don't forget, I had a part in the trial too. If not for me and my accent, the jury would have accepted Wendy's identification of Sanchez.

"Everyone involved with that case feels alone and desolate. But let me tell you the same thing I told each of them. They didn't set those men free, the law set them free. Their integrity is intact, no matter what the law did. You're suffering too. I've heard what everybody's saying about you, and I've tried to explain, but I'm just one voice crying out in the wilderness. But remember, although maybe you could foresee what would happen as a result of your actions, your actions were pure. The onus is on the law, on the men who created the law, and on the men today who through blindness refuse to change the law."

I shook my head. "Ed, I can't throw off all responsibility on the shoulders of others. I'm a free agent who chose to do certain things, in spite of my knowledge of the consequences."

"Well, John, maybe you have personal doubts. But I have no doubts about you. God may not approve of the exclusionary rule, but I know he approves of you."

I smiled a little. "Thank you, Bishop."

"You're welcome, Bishop."

I went home and climbed into bed, but I didn't sleep. My mind was too full of excited thoughts.

The next morning, Heber called me up from the jail and told me that the oil company's lawyer would handle the case so that there was no use in me coming over. I then asked Paul if he wanted to go with me up to Fairview for a little while.

"Sure," he agreed.

"John, Paul has to go to school," Carol protested.

"He's needed worse by me than by the school. I'll get him back before third period, easily."

"If we're late, it's OK," Paul said. He was willing to perform any sacrifice for his father.

"Why are you going?" Carol asked, still perturbed.

"I'll tell you later when I get back. I have to check something first."

Paul and I drove away. "Paul, are there any merit badges involving a visit to an oil drilling operation?"

"I think so."

"Why don't you work on that merit badge?"

"OK, I guess. But first I have to find out which one it is."

We went past Fairview and up into the mountains where oil drilling crews had been working away. There was a roadblock on one of the private roads.

"Hello, sir, what can I do for you?" a smiling guard asked.

"My boy here is after a merit badge. We'd like to see the oil rigs."

The guard shook his head, but he was really nice. "I'm sorry, but at the moment, I'm not supposed to let anyone through. But come back late next week and I'll give you a guided tour myself, answer any questions I can, and find out the answers that I don't know."

I thanked him, and we returned to Ammon. Paul didn't ask me what I was doing. I took him to school before the first period was over, then I drove back north again, stopping at the big trailer court in Fairview. I talked to the owner, who had long been trying to sell the court so he could retire. Then I went to Brent Crenshaw's office.

"Hello, John, what can I do for you?"

"What are the names of the heirs who inherited that farm just outside of town?"

"The Rasmussen place?"

"Yeah."

"Jack Rasmussen and Lark Rasmussen Anderson."

"Where do they live?"

"California. Jack lives in—where?—Liverpool, Livermore, something like that. Lark and her husband live in Van Nuys. I have their addresses and phone numbers, if you want them. Have you found a buyer?"

"Maybe."

"Well, the property's just sat there for two years now, ever since Brother Rasmussen died. When interest rates were reasonable, the heirs were asking too much for it. Now that they're sky-high, they can't get rid of it. The property taxes are eating them up, they say. They're willing to sell for a lot less than market value, just to keep from having to pay the taxes. But from what I've heard, they haven't even had a nibble."

"Does it have water rights?"

"Plenty of water."

His secretary got me the phone numbers and addresses. Then I went home, called Jack Rasmussen, identified myself, and asked him how much he wanted for the farm. He told me. I could have dickered and probably forced the price down, but I didn't. "Mr. Rasmussen, you're aware that that is far below market value?"

"Not when there isn't any market."

"Mr. Rasmussen, I'm willing to buy it from you for that price, but first I want to tell you something that might change your mind. I have reason to suspect that oil has been found in Sanpete County."

"On my land?" he asked excitedly.

"No, nowhere near your land. But Fairview is the nearest town. If there is a big oil boom in the near future, the value of the land might rise if Fairview creeps over in your farm's direction. It could eventually be worth considerably more than you're asking."

"Why are you telling me this?"

"So you don't think I'm taking advantage of you. On the other hand, I'm not sure that oil has been discovered—I just have some clues. And for all I know, the oil might be too deep for economic recovery at today's oil prices, and they might not drill any more wells. But I don't know. I just want you to know all the options."

"So none of this is certain?"

"No, none of it is certain. But I'm willing to take the risk. If nothing else, I'll have a big farm."

"Can you have the money by the first of next week?"

"If you and your sister come up and sign, I'll have it by Tuesday."

"So what you're saying is that *if* we hold onto the land, and *if* oil has been discovered, and *if* it is economical, then our land *might* someday be worth more than it is now. So we might get rich, but if it busts, then we're still holding a big farm that we can't sell and that's taking our tax money."

"That's a pretty fair summary of the situation."

"I'm sick of the place. We'll be at your office next Tuesday."

I went home, talked to Carol, and afterwards called Lisa's father, who runs a dairy. Then I went to see a banker about mortgages. In the early afternoon I visited Bob Collingham at his bank.

"What can I do for you, John?"

"I need some money."

"How much?"

He whistled when I told him. "Are you going to put your house and duplexes up for collateral?"

"I mortgaged them to the hilt this morning."

"What're you going to buy with the money?"

"The Rasmussen place in Fairview."

"The Rasmussen place? John, it's been sitting there for two years. What're you going to do with it?"

"I'm going to build homes. The county won't let me practice law, so I'll build."

"If the county won't give you their business, what makes you think they'll buy homes from you?"

"I'll sell to newcomers," I replied.

"The county's growing, but not that fast. Why not start small, work your way up?"

"I'll put alfalfa on most of the land until I build on it. I called Lisa's dad, and he said he'd do the planting and cutting and buy it all from me, if I take care of the watering. He's getting it at a good price, so it'll benefit us both. He needs a lot for his dairy."

"But John, the money from the alfalfa won't make your payments."

"Look, they're selling it well below market value."

"There's no market value if there is no market. No one can afford to buy that much acreage with today's interest rates. If the bank has to foreclose, we'll find ourselves owning a white elephant."

"Bob, I'll make the payments."

"I believe that you believe that you'll make the payments, but good intentions don't count. You have no law practice. If you had one, then maybe that would take care of your cash flow problem. I'm sorry, John, the answer is no. It's a half-baked scheme of desperation. You won't be able to sell the homes; you probably won't even get financing to build homes. You're my friend, but in this office I work for this bank, and I'm holding all these funds in trust for our depositors. I'm sorry, John."

"They discovered oil," I replied.

I got my loan.

Next I called my big brother. "Ryan, this is your baby brother."

"Hello, Johnny!"

"How would you like to go into partnership with me in developing a subdivision here in Sanpete County?"

"Oh, not very much."

"Then how about arranging for some construction loans for me?"

"In Sanpete County? You guys've got one of the highest unemployment rates in the state. There's no one there with enough money to buy homes."

"Ryan, they've discovered oil."

"Oh."

I described my plan. If there were a building boom, builders would flock to Fairview. I would be just one of many. However, I had mortgaged my home and duplexes to buy the trailer court. It had cost more than it was worth—I could have built a new one cheaper—but I couldn't afford the time. The court would set me apart from all other builders. I could offer incoming families a place to stay while building their homes. Housing would be at a premium in a small town like Fairview. The court came complete with seven trailers, plus thirty-five trailer lots that were developed but presently unoccupied. Since I had bought the farm land so cheaply, I could sell lots cheaply, and I could get subcontractors to knock down their prices in return for a guarantee of consecutive houses to work on. I could sell inexpensively, but since I lived in the county, I wanted to put up well-built homes that wouldn't turn into a slum. I wasn't sure how many oilmen would come to Sanpete County, but it wouldn't take many to keep me afloat. It was ironic that the same court case that cost me my law practice had given me such a reputation for sharp dealing that the DUI suspect in jail had asked for me, giving me a clue to the oil discovery.

Ryan laughed. "You've really come up with something, haven't you? It's about time you quit that Mickey Mouse law practice and started doing something worthwhile. I'll cosign with you on some construction loans. But Johnny, what if the oil isn't economical to get out? That'll kill your little scheme, won't it?"

"I'll have a few sales anyway. They'll leave a maintenance crew here for what they've already dug. They've been living in the motels so far. Since they'll be staying, they'll want to bring their families here, so I'll get a few sales. Even with no big boom I should come out of this owning the farm free and clear. That's something, at least. And the trailer court will give me a constant stream of cash."

Ryan liked the scheme. It's nice to have a wealthy brother. This was the first time I had taken advantage of his help, though he had kept me employed while I was in school. Ryan had a credit rating so good that every time he pulled into a bank's parking lot, the prime interest rate fell.

I was relieved that I'd no longer have to depend on the goodwill of my neighbors for a living, at least for a while. Undoubtedly, some of them would be disappointed to see that I didn't dry up and blow away. But that was their problem, not mine. I bore them no ill will.

That evening our Scoutmaster, Joshua Erickson, was at a court of honor with his family when his home was burglarized. No money was missing, since they had none in the house, but an AM/FM-cassette tape recorder was taken, and a great deal of damage was done.

The community panicked. Previously the biggest crime wave Ammon had ever suffered was when two shopliftings occurred in one month at the 7-Eleven.

The next night I also received a phone call from the stake president. He wondered if I could come over to the stake offices. I said I'd be there in five minutes.

"Who was that?" Carol asked.

"President Fitzgerald."

Carol got tense. She gave me a kiss, and I left. I had never been afraid of facing the stake president before, but tonight, I went with trepidation. When I drove up to the stake offices, most of the lights were out since it was a Friday evening. I knocked on President Fitzgerald's door.

"Come in," came the muffled reply.

I entered. He held out his hand for me to shake, but he didn't smile.

"Hello, President."

"Hello, John. I'm releasing you from your calling as bishop."

Chapter Twenty-One

I had been expecting it; I had prepared myself to hear it; I had steeled myself against it; but it still hit me hard. I slumped down in my chair. "Oh."

He put his hand on his desk. He picked up a pen and toyed with it. "I want you to know that this has nothing to do with . . . recent events."

"OK."

"After all, you've served for over five-and-a-half years. I don't normally ask a bishop to serve more than five."

"I know."

He unscrewed the pen unconsciously. He tipped it, and the pieces fell out on the table. He looked at me. "Last January, because your five years were up, I decided to release you. But the Lord said no. The night after the trial, I decided to release you, but the Lord again said no. Yesterday President Tuttle and his family moved to Denver, and the Lord told me to release you."

He pushed the little pen spring with his finger, and it rolled across his desk. It stopped just before it fell off the edge. He bowed his head for a moment, then looked at the wall. "John, I want you to be my second counselor to replace President Tuttle. No, that's not true," he corrected, shaking his head. "I don't want you to be my second counselor. The Lord wants you to be my second counselor."

I caught my breath. I couldn't reply—I was absolutely stunned.

"You'll be getting a phone call from Salt Lake. They'll interview you and officially extend the calling to you. My telling you previously isn't exactly in accordance with Church policy, but I need to talk to you."

He was silent for a moment.

"I have some repenting to do, John. President and Sister Wainsgaard were some of my dearest friends. My nephew married their granddaughter. I was second counselor to President Wainsgaard. When the Lord told me last night who was to replace President Tuttle, I was . . . flabbergasted. I don't mind admitting it. I just happened to run into Kurt Vanderhoft today. Or maybe it was arranged. At any rate, he might not be active in the Church, but he is an intelligent man. I asked him about you. After all, I was pretty shaken up. He praised you up and down for half an hour, even though he was your opponent at the trial. He told me all kinds of things to justify what you did. I'm not a lawyer, John. I don't remember half of what he told me. They sounded reasonable when I heard them, but now . . . I just don't know. The bottom line is, two great people are dead, Wendy Wainsgaard is a blind orphan, seven Coombs kids have no father, and the murderers are free to murder again. The Lord wants you—and I've got to humble myself and learn to want you too. Last January, I was considering you as President Tuttle's replacement. But the night of the trial, I changed my mind. To be perfectly frank, if a mob had gathered outside your home that night, I might not have helped them throw stones, but I would have held their coats."

When I opened the front door at home, a quiet fell on the house. Carol, Lisa, Paul, Cindy, Susie, Sean, Jenny, and Johnny watched me as I came in and sat down heavily on the couch. Carol turned off the TV. I slumped down and looked at the ceiling.

"Did you get released from the bishopric?" Carol asked quietly.

I nodded my head slightly.

"Well, you put in your five years," Lisa said gently. "It was time for your release."

I nodded again.

"I'm glad!" Cindy said viciously. Hostile eyes turned to her. She went wordlessly to her room.

"I guess I'm kind of glad too," Carol admitted. "We'll see more of you from now on. It'll be nice having a husband again that's all mine and not shared with five hundred people in the ward."

I took my eyes from the ceiling. I could not keep up the pretense much longer.

"Are you moving now?" Lisa asked.

"Carol, can I talk to you?" I rose and went outside. Carol followed me into the darkness. I put my arm around her shoulders. The walnut trees were silhouetted clearly in the half-moonlight. I sat down on the bench and guided her onto my lap. "Sweetheart, I know how badly you wanted me to be released, but can you live without a full-time husband for a few more years?"

"What?"

"I'm going to be called as second counselor in the presidency of the Manti Utah Stake, The Church of Jesus Christ of Latter-day Saints."

She gave a girlish whoop of delight and excitedly kissed me. "See, I told you so! I told you so, didn't I?" she exclaimed.

"No, you didn't, you weren't expecting this any more than I was."

"I told you everything would work out, didn't I?" She gave me such a tight squeeze that I had difficulty breathing.

"Hey, watch it. Don't damage sacred property," I cautioned.

"John, I never expected it! I never thought that you . . ." Her voice trailed off.

I laughed. "Go ahead, say it. You never thought that someone like me would ever be in a stake presidency. Neither did I.

I never thought I'd be a bishop either. Or a counselor in a bishopric. I never wanted any of those callings. But though it sounds conceited, I did a pretty fair job as bishop. In my own opinion, I'm not stake presidency caliber, but the Lord expects a man to grow gradually into the job."

"Let's tell the kids," Carol said eagerly.

"No. I'm not supposed to spread it around too much before stake conference next week. Paul won't tell, but Susie might accidentally let it slip out, and Cindy would scream it from the housetops if she thought it would increase her status. We can write and tell Matthew, though. He won't get the letter until conference is over anyway. It wouldn't be fair to tell Paul and not tell the other kids."

"You've got to tell Lisa," Carol implored.

"Carol, for a long time now my counselors and my secretary have known things that my wife didn't get to hear. For just this once, I want to let the others wait a few days and just share this secret with the woman I love. OK?"

Carol smiled and kissed me. I picked her up in my arms and carried her back to the house.

Chapter Twenty-Two

On Saturday, the rumor was allowed to leak that there would be a reorganization of the bishopric. They always do that. It guarantees a full house at church, and so it proved Sunday. The chapel was filled, the overflow was full, and we even had to open the sliding partition between the overflow and the gym to handle the crowd. Afterward, Tom Kanagawa told me that we had an attendance of 218 percent. Most of the First Ward was in attendance at our Second Ward meeting. Bishop Alvirez was going to be lonely. I recognized people from Ephraim, Manti, and Sterling. People always flock to see a public pillory.

For the last time, I conducted the opening of the meeting. After the opening hymn and invocation, I conducted some ward business, and then turned the time over to President Fitzgerald.

"We are here today to reorganize your bishopric," he announced. "Bishop Lindsey has done an outstanding job for over five-and-a-half years. Those who can now join us in a vote of thanks to Bishop Lindsey for a job well done, show it by the uplifted hand."

It was such a small gesture to make, the only official thanks one receives for years of sacrifice. Perhaps my bitterness can be excused when I saw most of the people in the congregation suddenly get involved in cautioning kids who had not been unruly, picking up hymnbooks, and fussing with scriptures. Perhaps one hundred and fifty people raised their hands.

It suddenly occurred to me that in spite of the fact that I had been called to join the stake presidency, I would not be set apart in that position unless the congregation at stake conference raised their hands to sustain my calling. All things must be done by common consent, and it was not a foregone conclusion that I would receive that consent.

As church let out, I noticed a look of triumph in the eyes of some members. Perhaps justice didn't always prevail in the courts of our land, but in the Church, truth and justice were always victorious. I had been put in my place.

The next week I spent a lot of time in Fairview, consulting with city officials, getting permits, hiring surveyors, draftsmen, and engineers, and fixing up house trailers. By Wednesday, all my house trailers and two vacant lots were rented to oilmen who needed a place to stay or to put the trailers they were going to bring. Several discreetly asked me whether I knew of any nice homes for a good price. I mentioned that some well-built homes at a low price would shortly be constructed in a new subdivision. They said they'd keep me in mind.

My brother, Ryan, came from Salt Lake, looked over my plans, and pronounced them good. He made some helpful suggestions, and most importantly he cosigned on the construction loans.

Thursday night there was another burglary. Brother and Sister Adams, the heads of the the ward activities committee in the First Ward, had their house hit. They were in charge of a ward dinner at the time.

It was becoming obvious that these were inside jobs, done by someone who knew our town and the people in it well enough to know when the families definitely would not be home.

Saturday was Mark's birthday. We went a little further than financial prudence dictated to get gifts for Mark. Cindy jealously told Carol that before her next birthday she was going to mope around all the time so that we'd bribe her with gifts too. Mark, however, appeared totally unmoved by the pleasant party

Brenda threw for him, and he opened the gifts we gave him with no enthusiasm. After the cake and ice cream, he went to his room. I considered asking him what his plans for the summer were, since he was now a high school graduate. I wasn't going to let him brood in his room all summer long. But I was still a little bit too unsure of myself to risk another confrontation.

On Saturday afternoon, word leaked out that the stake presidency would be reorganized the next day. Again, attendance at stake conference soared as the faithful and the curious flocked from Manti, Ephraim, Sterling, and Ammon. Carol and Brenda prevailed upon Mark to come. Though Mark was still moody and uncommunicative, the nature of his condition had changed. His previous rebellion seemed to have been replaced by simple depression.

After the opening hymn and prayer, President Fitzgerald announced that because of his employment, President Tuttle had to be released from his calling as second counselor. He told us all how much we would miss President Tuttle and his family, then asked for a vote of thanks. Everyone I could see but Mark raised his hand in the vote of appreciation. Mark was leaning forward, his elbows on his knees, his palms supporting his head, as he stared at the floor.

"Brother Lindsey, could you come up to the stand, please?"

I was sitting at the back of the crowded gym with my family. Carol beamed, and Lisa looked at me with delighted astonishment. Mark raised his head and gazed at me with wonder as I stood up. The building became suddenly silent, no small accomplishment for a Mormon congregation. My footsteps reverberated loudly throughout the gym, stopping when I entered the carpeted overflow. I continued up the chapel aisle. Eyes were wide open and mouths were agape on both sides of the aisle. I sprang up the three steps to the stand, and President Fitzgerald motioned me next to his side. I was considerably taller than he was, but he reached up and put his hand on my shoulder.

"The Lord has called Brother Lindsey to be my second

counselor." He paused for a moment, gave me a comical sideways glance, and added, "Don't ask me why."

The congregation laughed, and some of the tension was eased.

He continued. "We mortals tend to judge by appearances, but—" His voice suddenly choked up. He stood still for a moment, leaning on my shoulder. ". . . but the Lord judges by the heart," he finally said in a husky voice. "Those who can join me in sustaining Brother John Jacob Lindsey as the second counselor in the stake presidency of the Manti Utah Stake of The Church of Jesus Christ of Latter-day Saints, please show it by the uplifted hand." He vigorously raised his hand.

His vigor was not matched by the congregation. Hands slowly appeared throughout the church. President Fitzgerald meaningfully thrust his hand even higher, and more people in the congregation responded. Eventually, most of the members raised their hands. It was hard to see at first, but by squinting I managed to see Mark. He was not raising his hand, though Cindy was raising hers enthusiastically.

"Those opposed, show it by the same sign."

About thirty people in the congregation got up and walked out. Adney Cannest was among them. The president waited until they had filed out, but no one raised his hand in opposition.

"Thank you," he said. "President Lindsey, could you take the seat to the left of mine? The sheep on my right hand, the goat on my left." Everybody laughed again. I sat down, and President Simons, the first counselor, reached over and shook my hand. The business completed, President Fitzgerald continued with his remarks. But the congregation wasn't looking at him— they were all staring at me. I knew it would be hard for them for a while, but I was grateful to them for the fact that, though they did not comprehend, they had enough faith to sustain me. At least, very few were actively against me.

While we were driving home in the station wagon, Cindy hoped out loud that all her friends had been to conference.

Brenda lay bets that I would be stake president in five years. I fervently hoped she was wrong and said so. Susie, Sean, and Jenny rhythmically chanted, "President Lindsey, President Lindsey," until Cindy told them to shut up. Paul said, "Way to go, Dad."

Only Mark said nothing. As he got out of the car, I noticed he had tears in his eyes.

When I came home from Fairview on Monday afternoon, Carol waved a little piece of paper under my nose as I entered the house.

"What's that?"

"You've had four phone calls today, people wanting some legal work done. I took the names down for you. And Kerry at Betty's Home Cooking called about one o'clock. He said that several people had been to the office and when they didn't find anyone there, they asked Kerry when you'd be back. I called Lisa at the store, and she's over at the office right now. You'd better go check with her. She quit the store. I *told* you things would work out!" Carol was nice in that way. She never said "I told you so" when you did something stupid; she only said it when it made you feel good.

"How are things going in Fairview?"

"Really nice. The city is cooperative, and there're so many construction men without work that I don't have to wait for anything. I think the first four homes could be ready to move into by August and four more right after that."

"Pretty tight schedule."

"Everybody's cooperating. I already have three signed contracts and earnest money for three houses, and I haven't even put in the foundations yet. I leased another trailer lot today. If all eight houses sell, we'll be able to repay our debt and get our house out of hock. So whatever else happens, we'll own the farm free and clear as well as the trailer park. Even if a big boom doesn't come, we'll be better off than we were six months ago." I took her in my arms. "Thanks for letting me mortgage your home out from under you."

"That was quite a gamble you took, risking our house on the word of three drunk oilmen and a guard who wouldn't let you onto the premises."

"Well, Sister Riches, the den mother, told me two weeks ago that she had taken her den to the oil rigs and that the guard had been really nice and had showed them all over the place. The guard was still nice, but the fact that he wouldn't let me in made me realize that something was going on."

"Well, at the time it looked like pretty slim evidence to me."

"Yes, I guess I exercised pretty good judgment in this situation. But then, I've always had better judgment than you."

"You have not," Carol countered, slightly hurt.

"Sure, I have." I smiled. "For example, look at who I married compared to who you married."

Carol laughed, then gave me a warm kiss.

When I arrived at the office, Lisa was already there, wearing one of her nicest outfits. I asked how things were going.

"Five people came in this afternoon," Lisa reported. "There was another call on the answering machine. You'd better return their calls," she said with a big smile.

"Get tired of Foodtown?"

"Not really, but I didn't want to miss out on all the action. Chuck was impressed with my work. He said I'd done really well, even though I wasn't there for long. And he said that my presence greatly boosted the number of male customers," she stated with the complacent vanity that is typical of Annie Lindsey's descendants.

"Sounds like you've learned humility from me," I commented. "And it's no wonder that all the guys swarmed to the store if you dressed like that every day."

"I had a hunch that I wouldn't be spending all day at the store, so I put on my favorite dress so I'd look nice for your flood of clients."

"Well, I never expected it," I admitted.

"I did. When President Fitzgerald choked up on the stand

yesterday, I wanted to cry too, even though I hadn't done any-thing mean to you. I think lots of people felt the same way. You see, we Mormons are very big on the 'fallen angel' syndrome. We naturally think that when a man is called to a Church posi-tion, the Lord has found him worthy. But we have learned by sad experience that a worthy man can be corrupted while con-tinuing to hold his position. I'm sure most people figured that the cares of the world had gotten to you and you'd become a fallen bishop. Even though you attorneys have a high regard for yourselves and your honesty, most people are slightly afraid and distrustful of lawyers. I imagine that most of your clients saw the results of the trial and figured you were just another corrupt attorney who had no regard for right and wrong. But since most of the people in this county believe that the Lord called you to the stake presidency, they figure that he must be vouching for your character.

"It's human nature to kick a dog when he's down. But it's also human nature to try to make it up to him when he's been wronged."

"Well, Sigmund Freud, do you have those numbers for me to call?" I asked.

She gave them to me. The telephone call on the answering machine was from an attorney in Ogden, not from a local client. I dialed her first. A secretary came on the phone, and I iden-tified myself. A moment later, the attorney came on the phone.

"Mr. Lindsey? This is Jill Hasbro. I've been representing Mr. Russell Montague. He isn't satisfied with my conclusions as to his chances, and he wanted me to call you and ask you to repre-sent him."

"What's happened to him?"

"He's been arrested for possession of and attempting to sell over one hundred thousand dollars worth of cocaine and a small amount of heroin. The police claim that they have vid-eotapes, marked money, the works. I can't find a hole in their case. But Mr. Montague refuses to plea bargain. He says some-thing will turn up. He wants you for the case."

"How about entrapment?"

"I'll argue it, naturally, but we don't have a chance. Still, he says you got him off in the last case when he didn't have a chance there either."

"Tell Mr. Montague that I'm pretty busy right now."

"He says to tell you that money is no object. He has recently done quite well in business, and you can name your price."

I knew very well what business he'd have to be involved in to get a lot of money in such a short time. I could really have used the fee from a big felony defense case, but I was not unduly tempted. "He can't afford my price," I replied. "But thank you for calling." I hung up the phone.

While in my youth, I'd spent the summer once with my mother's family in Tennesee. One of my uncles had taught me the rebel yell. That was one of the reasons Mom had sent me to live with Lisa's parents the following year. Though Mom had cured me of my yell, I hadn't forgotten—"YEE-AAY-EEE!"

"Good heavens!" Lisa cried. "What on earth—"

"They busted Montague! They got him! The narcs nailed him!"

She laughed merrily and jumped up from her chair.

"I'm going to tell Kurt. He'll want to know," I said excitedly. "Can I borrow your car?"

"If you take me along."

As we whizzed by some tall bushes on the side of the road, Lisa noticed Chief Reitzen's patrol car. I slammed on the brakes, backed up to his car, and Lisa shouted out the window, "They got Montague! They busted him for drugs!"

The chief flashed us the victory sign and a smile, and we took off.

We parked the car and ran together to Kurt's office.

"Can we talk to Kurt?" I asked his secretary, Gwen.

Just then, Kurt opened his inner office door and saw our faces. "What are you two so happy about?" he asked genially.

"They caught Montague on a drug charge," Lisa said breathlessly.

"Really?" He laughed. "That's great!"

"His attorney called me, says they've got him nailed," I explained. "Hundred thousand worth of coke. Videotapes, the works."

"That deserves a drink!" Kurt announced.

He went into his inner office and came out bearing two Pepsis and two Sprites.

"None of this sinful stuff for you, Prez," he said, handing me a Sprite. "That's quite a promotion. I propose a toast," he proclaimed. "To Russell Montague. May he rot in jail forever!"

I took a sip of Sprite and hiccuped.

"Too strong for you, Prez?" he asked.

I nodded. We silently consumed our drinks.

Suddenly, Kurt slammed his drink to the floor. "We should have had them!" he roared. The can hit the floor and rolled, leaving a trail of cola as it went. It finally hit the wall and stayed there, the dark liquid pulsing out and forming an ever-increasing puddle. We watched the puddle swell until the can emptied itself.

"One to fifteen is better than nothing," I said quietly.

"He'll be out in two years. Three years, max. The board of pardons isn't allowed to consider a murder for which he wasn't convicted!"

"They're human—they might keep him there fifteen years."

Kurt shook his head. "Possible equal protection problems, not to mention prison overcrowding. In three years, he'll be out. We'll eventually get him, but only after he's killed again, or-phaned a few more kids." With a violent lunge, he kicked the side of the secretary's desk. "John, that exclusionary rule is in-sane! It's crazy to let guys like them go!"

"Well, we need something to keep the police from ha-rassing people illegally," Lisa observed.

Kurt looked at her fiercely. But after a moment, his face softened. It was hard to look at Lisa and be angry.

"Has your secretary been reading *Mapp v. Ohio*?" he asked

with a bitter smile. "Sure, I quote it too, but only to the ignorant. The Supreme Court only fashioned the exclusionary rule because there was no remedy to offer people whose Fourth Amendment rights had been violated by illegal search and seizures. The court says that the purpose of the rule is to discourage officers from violating the Fourth Amendment, like Lisa said. But if that's the purpose of it, they've certainly found an idiotic way to do it. Throwing out the evidence that was illegally seized does nothing to punish the bad cop, but it does usually free the criminal. It means that society can't punish the lawbreaker because of the activities of another lawbreaker who happens to be wearing a uniform. If the police harass a good person who hasn't done anything, the fact that a court can't use illegally seized evidence means nothing because the good folks haven't committed a crime and won't face a court. It doesn't protect the innocent from bad cops, just the guilty.

"The U.S. Justice Department commissioned Dallin Oaks to study the effects of the exclusionary rule, and he found no evidence to suggest that it detered cops. He suggested a viable alternative to the rule. Chief Justice Burger and others have also come up with viable alternatives. Our gutsy Utah legislature just passed a law that hopes to soften the effects of the exclusionary rule. It says that if the cop's actions were in good faith or the violations were minor, then the exclusionary rule won't apply. That's better than nothing, I guess. But a rule like the one they just passed wouldn't have helped in Montague's case. Frost was a rogue cop—there was no good faith on his part. But why should we be punished for something he did? The law has to be tested before the U.S. Supreme Court anyway, so why not go all the way and eliminate the exclusionary rule altogether, replacing it with something better?"

"I read where only a small percentage of crooks are released because of the exclusionary rule, so it wouldn't stop the crime wave to do away with it," Lisa commented.

"That's like saying Pol Pot wasn't very bad because he killed only two million of his fellow Cambodians, which represents just a small percentage of earth's total population," Kurt replied. "In Oaks's study, nearly half of all gambling cases, a third of all narcotics cases, and a fourth of all illegal weapons cases were thrown out of Chicago courts because of the exclusionary rule, showing that it doesn't deter cops or benefit anyone but the crooks.

"We've got to get rid of the exclusionary rule. It doesn't work. England and Canada are just as free as we are and have similar justice systems, but they manage without an exclusionary rule. We've got to stop thinking that that rule is holy. The Constitution doesn't require it, no matter what nine old men said years ago, and it did not come down from Mount Sinai on stone tablets. We can change it."

"Why haven't we?" Lisa asked.

"Inertia," I replied.

Kurt laughed bitterly. "Yeah, inertia—an object at rest tends to remain at rest. Congress has been at rest too long, but it surely has enough latent wisdom to get something done if it chooses to do so. There's something wrong with a system where, if a crook and a cop both break the law, they both get off scot free.

"I don't pretend to know everything. I'm just a hick lawyer in a hick county of a hick state. But I know justice when I see it, and we aren't getting justice."

Kurt reached down and picked up the empty can. He threw it into the pile he was saving for the Cub Scouts. Gwen was about to get some paper towels, but Kurt said no, he wanted to look at the puddle.

As suddenly as it had left, Kurt's good humor returned. "John, did you hear about Nick Hansen?"

"No."

"Judge Hastings turned him in for refusing to accept a court appointment for political reasons. And especially for bad-mouthing the attorney who finally took over the appointment he refused."

"Really? What do you think they'll do to him?"

"With that official reproval he got last year, I figure they might suspend him. It'll be funny if he wins the election for county attorney and finds himself unable to practice."

The next morning I was explaining to Lisa some changes I needed made in a document when the office phone rang.

"John Lindsey's office. Can I help you?" Lisa answered. "Oh, hello," she said flatly. "Yes, it's been a while. No, I don't think so. But if you'd like to come over Sunday night and talk, I'll listen. I put the kids in bed at eight. Anytime after that. Fine. Goodbye." Her mouth had been taut with suppressed anger as she talked, but when she hung up the phone, her voice had more sorrow in it than anger. "That was Leonard," she reported.

"What'd he have to say?"

She pushed the phone away. "He said he'd like to redeem his raincheck, take me out to dinner and a movie, and take the kids to the Alpine slide on Saturday."

"You turned him down?"

She nodded. "But I told him I'd talk to him. That's more than he'd do for me. When I was the cousin of the town untouchable, he deserted me. Now that I'm the cousin of a member of the stake presidency, he's back." She looked down at the desk for a moment. "When I needed his support so badly, he wasn't there. He's certainly not a Lindsey, is he?"

I said nothing.

"But I'll listen to him," she continued. "He was a neat guy, Johnny. Maybe he can say something Sunday night that will take away the bitterness."

Paul burst through the front door. "Hey, Dad!" he said excitedly. "Have you seen the *Advocate* yet?"

"Not yet."

"What does it say?" Lisa asked.

"Mr. Vanderhoft wrote a long letter to the editor about you. It says that Montague would have escaped from jail, but you used your karate to knock him out and hold him for the police."

"Judo," I corrected. "And he couldn't have gotten away anyway, and I didn't knock him out. I just slammed him to the ground and got him in a wrist lock."

"Kurt ought to get together with Aunt Harriet," Lisa said. "They could write up the definitive version of your life."

"It says that after you subdued Montague, he asked you whose side you were on and you said, 'The law's side,'" Paul continued happily. "Mr. Vanderhoft says you were a hero through the whole thing."

Lisa took the *Ammon Advocate* from Paul. "Yep, you're a hero. Says so right here in black and white," she remarked with a twinkle in her eye.

"I heard that Judge Hastings wrote letters to the editors of the *Manti Messenger*, the *Ephraim Enterprise,* the Gunnison paper, and the Mount Pleasant paper," Paul added. "I saw the *Enterprise* about an hour ago. The judge said how you did what you had to do, and gave a really good explanation of the whole thing."

Lisa handed me the paper. On the front page was a picture of me next to a story about the reorganization of the stake presidency. I wondered if the letters would have been written if not for the front page story. Kurt and the judge certainly waited until I was no longer a hot subject before they stuck up for me. Nevertheless, I was grateful.

"Well, John Jacob Lindsey the Third, I guess society has rehabilitated another dangerous criminal," Lisa teased.

I sat down on the edge of Lisa's desk. I shook my head. "I've got my reputation back, sure. But nothing is resolved."

"What do you mean?" she asked.

I tried to formulate my thoughts. "I don't know. Everyone seems to have the idea that because the Lord called me to the stake presidency, he must approve of what went on and what I did. I just can't accept that. All he did was call me to the stake presidency—he didn't put his seal of approval on anything."

"I'm sure the Lord realizes you had to do what you did," Lisa said.

"I didn't *have* to do anything. I could have refused to take part if I were willing to accept the consequences that the state would have inflicted on me."

"Johnny, don't start blaming yourself for what happened."

"I'm not. But I recall when Joseph Smith disobeyed the Lord's counsel by giving the first 116 pages of the Book of Mormon to a wicked man. He ended up losing them. The Lord withdrew from Joseph, and for a while Joseph lost his gift of translation. Later, the Lord restored the gift to him, but that doesn't mean the Lord approved of what Joseph had done. It meant that the Lord had forgiven him."

"So you think it's the same in your case?" Lisa inquired.

"I don't know. I'm sure the Lord couldn't approve of what happened in that trial, but I don't know if he tolerated my part in it or holds me accountable for it. I didn't disobey the counsel of God because this is one subject he chose not to discuss with me. He left me on my own. I still don't understand why. But I have faith in him, even when I don't understand him." I looked down at the picture of myself in the paper. "Kind of funny, isn't it?" I mused. "I haven't changed a bit in the last few weeks, but I was a bum before, and now I'm a hero."

"You've changed," Lisa replied. "You couldn't help but change. Fire burns wood but tempers steel. This shows which you were made of."

Paul grinned. "Careful, Dad, sounds like she's buttering you up for a raise."

That evening there was a dinner at the ward. Though Mark refused to come with us, I still looked forward to attending a church dinner in which I had no responsibilities.

After the dinner, while we were waiting for the entertainment, Sister Kanagawa called out to me. "Raising a kleptomaniac, John?" she asked smiling and pointing to Johnny. He was emptying her purse, examining the contents.

"Johnny!" Carol called. He looked up and came to her, bringing Sister Kanagawa's compact with him. He proudly displayed his trophy to Carol and Lisa.

"Take it back to Sister Kanagawa, Johnny," Carol said. Johnny obediently toddled back to Sister Kanagawa and gallantly offered her the compact. He ran back into Carol's arms to be extravagantly praised.

"Johnny can walk really well now," Lisa observed.

I nodded. "But he wouldn't be this far along if we'd kept making everything easy for him."

A little girl walked up to me. "President, Uncle Heber wants to talk to you. He's out there," she pointed.

"Thank you, Sally, " I said and walked out to meet the police chief.

Chief Reitzen was waiting for me in the foyer. He motioned for me to go outside with him.

Out in the warm night air, he waited for a moment while the door slowly closed behind us. The expression on his face alarmed me even before he spoke. "John, a burglary was attempted at the MacDonalds' house. We caught two boys, Chris Brinkman and Arnie Smith. We saw another boy run off in the direction of your house. Arnie isn't saying much right now— he's just gone to pieces and he's bawling like a baby. But Chris . . ." He paused a moment and looked at me with pity. "Chris says that the other boy was Mark."

Chapter Twenty-Three

I was glad that Heber was there to lean on as the blood drained from my head. He put out a strong hand and steadied me.

"Heber," I said finally in a strained voice, "are you sure?"

He handed me a Boy Scout pocketknife inside a plastic bag. "We found this at the window the boys were trying to force." Raggedly engraved on the knife blade was "MJ Lindsey": Mark Jacob Lindsey. I had given him the knife when he was a Tenderfoot Scout and had engraved it to keep it from getting mistaken with the other boys' knives.

"Chris ran over to your house when we turned on our lights. He was pounding on the door and cussing and yelling for Mark to let him in. We tried the doors, but they were all locked. Rather than break in, we surrounded the house, and I came for you. We got some deputies from the sheriff there, too. Could you let us in?"

I nodded weakly. We got into the police car and drove to my house. I let Heber and two county deputies into the house, while Ed Alvirez and another deputy kept a watch on the house from the outside.

My gallon canteen was missing from the camping gear, as well as my pair of binoculars. In the food storage area, all the blackberry fruit leather was gone. For an irrational instant, I was angrier at Mark for taking the rest of the fruit leather than for trying to steal from a neighbor who had been so good to us.

A frightening thought occurred to me. I rushed to a cabinet and threw it open. It was still there, my biggest memento from Vietnam—a 6.5 mm Arisaka rifle, the weapon that had equipped the Japanese infantry during World War II. I had taken it from a VC the night I escaped from my captors. It was the only firearm I owned, and Mark had known where it was and how to use it. I was immensely relieved to know that he hadn't taken it.

We searched the house thoroughly. I took the officers into the attic and showed them every conceivable place a person could hide in. Mark was no longer around.

When we went back outside, Carol, Lisa, and the kids drove up. The flashing red-and-blue lights added a hellish, surrealistic atmosphere to the yard.

"What on earth is going on?" Carol demanded. "Sister Williams down the street saw the lights and called the church."

"Did they burglarize your house tonight, Johnny?" Lisa asked.

"Some boys tried to break into the MacDonald house," Chief Reitzen explained. I wanted him to continue, but he didn't.

"Mark was one of them," I finally added.

Carol looked at me with angry incredulity. "Mark wouldn't do anything like that! Especially to the MacDonalds!"

But things were beginning to fit together for me. Mark's moroseness, bad temper, and tormenting of the other kids were obviously the result of a guilty conscience. Like me, he had long been an admirer of Brother MacDonald's immense coin collection. It was worth a lot, not to mention Sister MacDonald's antique silver service. Mark would never plan such a thing on his own, but ever since the trial, Chris seemed to have more influence over Mark than I had.

"They found Mark's knife by the window they were trying to jimmie open," I argued. Chief Reitzen showed her the knife, but she wouldn't take it.

232

"I don't care—I know he wouldn't do it."

"He ran away," I insisted. "And he took my big canteen and binoculars and all the blackberry fruit leather."

Carol didn't deign to reply. She went into the house. Our kids, with stunned expressions, followed her.

"I'm sorry, President," Heber muttered. "If Mark comes back or if he calls you, will you let us know?"

I nodded my head miserably. He and the other officers got into their vehicles, and one by one they drove away. Lisa, her kids, and I were left standing under the porch light. A cricket crept onto the lighted area of the sidewalk. I viciously tried to smash it but missed, and it hopped away into the darkness.

"Carol's right," Lisa said. "Maybe Mark would steal, though I doubt it. But he definitely wouldn't steal from the Mac-Donalds. They've been good to all of you. Mark is no ingrate, whatever else he might be."

"No? Look how he's treated his father for the past few months. Even if he didn't understand what I did, he should have at least had some faith in me. He still hasn't spoken to me civilly after all these weeks."

"He has your blood," Lisa replied. "He grew up watching you. He might have your faults. He's got your looks, so he'll probably get your vanity. And he might inherit your occasional splash of self-righteousness, not to mention your difficulty in forgiving those who've wronged you. He's sure showed your tendency to rush in and judge people you love before you have all the facts. But there is no thievery in the Lindsey blood—not in our line of it. Mark isn't a thief."

"Tell me, in your scientific evaluation of Lindsey family genetics, how do you account for Mark's laziness and his lack of ambition?" I asked with heavy sarcasm. "People aren't entirely a product of their genes or their upbringing. Unlike you and Carol, I just refuse to close my eyes to the facts. 'My kid can do no wrong' is what the mothers of the worst kids say."

"I won't argue with you, Johnny. I can't. The facts are against me, but I'm going to give Mark the benefit of what little doubt remains. You complain that Mark showed no faith in you. You're reciprocating." She was quiet for a moment.

"Twenty years ago when you left me, I gave you the benefit of the doubt. I refused to hate you despite the fact that it looked like you'd just toyed with me and then run off to get engaged to another girl a few months later. Eventually, I found that my faith in you was justified.

"You've tried the faith of us all in the last few months, Johnny. You freed a murderer. Carol told me how hard it was for her that evening. At the last minute, she decided that she loved you, so she had to trust you. Brenda and Paul and Susie and I all love you, so we had to give you the trust you'd earned from your actions all these years. You'd better be absolutely sure before you condemn Mark. He got the seeds of goodness by watching you. If you love him, you'd better have faith in him."

I gazed out into the darkness, not replying. Feeling hurt and betrayed, I was in no mood to listen.

"Well, goodnight, Johnny," Lisa said. "I can take care of the office alone tomorrow if you don't feel like coming."

"Johnny?" Sean asked.

"What?"

"Is Mark coming back?"

I said nothing.

"He's coming back, sweetheart," Lisa said. "Let's go home."

Sean told me goodnight, and Jenny gave me a kiss. I watched while the three of them walked together down the dark street to their home.

I went into the house. Everyone was silent. Susie wept quietly. I half expected Cindy to make some remark about how bad this would make her look at school, but she too sat quietly with tears on her cheeks. Paul asked if I wanted him to go out and look for Mark. I told him no. After family prayer, we all went to bed.

I undressed for bed and knelt down by Carol for my private prayer. She had started before me and continued after I had finished. I got into bed and watched her. After ten minutes she was still on her knees. Fifteen minutes passed, and she was still there. On my mission I would occasionally be so tired that I would fall asleep on my knees while praying. I wondered if Carol had fallen asleep. After twenty minutes, I brushed her hair with my hand. "Sweetheart?" I said softly.

She looked up at me alertly, then bowed her head again. I didn't bother her anymore. Ten minutes after I had spoken to her, she got into bed beside me. "My son wouldn't do something like that," she said, but from the trembling in her voice, it appeared that she was trying to convince herself more than me. I could have remarked that Mr. Sanchez had said the same thing about his son. But it would have been cruel, so I kept silent.

Lying quietly in bed, my legal instincts took over. Mark had just turned eighteen and was now legally an adult. For a first offense of this nature in Salt Lake, he might get probation. But Sanpete county had sent a man to prison for stealing a turkey. Tried in this county, Mark would go to prison.

After a while, Carol's regular breathing told me that she was asleep. She moaned lightly in her sleep once but turned over and was silent.

Sleep eluded me. I tried for a while to doze off but finally got up and got dressed. I walked outside to the walnut trees and sat on the bench. Two bats swooped into the porch light, circled frantically, and vanished into the night. Crickets chirped tauntingly from their hiding places.

Sons tend to follow the examples that their fathers set. Had Mark done anything worse than he'd seen his father do?

I was ashamed of the tears that crept down my cheeks. I wiped them off with my sleeve, and I prayed. I prayed for a son who didn't understand his father, and I prayed for a father who had been unsure of his duty. The moon rose and climbed, the warm night breeze rustled the leaves over my head, and still I prayed.

"Dad . . ."

I looked up. My son's head was silhouetted by the moon

above him. I rose on unsteady legs. The embrace I gave him was awkward because of the canteen and the binoculars that hung between us. Mark's face was moist, too.

My first thought was how to persuade him to turn himself in and face justice. "Mark . . ."

"Dad," he wept, "I turned them in! I turned my best friends in!"

I kept silent, wondering what he was talking about.

"I figured out a few weeks ago that Chris and the guys were the ones burglarizing those homes, but I just couldn't turn them in. Yesterday Chris told me that I had to help them get Brother MacDonald's coin collection. I told him that if he did, I would turn him in. I told him that if he did any more burglaries at all, I'd turn him in, but he didn't believe me. He said that all I had to do was stay in our house and let him and the guys in if anything went wrong, or if anyone was coming. I told him again I'd turn him in. He laughed and said that if I turned him in, he'd lie and tell the cops that I was in on it. So I called Bishop Alvirez and told him that the MacDonalds' house was going to be hit tonight."

"Did you tell him who you were?"

Mark shook his head. I put my arm around his shoulders, and we sat down together.

"As soon as you guys went to the dinner, I took a canteen, binoculars, and something to eat and went up to the family knoll and waited. I didn't want to be home when the guys came by. I didn't want to get mixed up in it at all. I saw the police lights flashing. I guess they got them."

I nodded. "They got Chris and Arnie. They saw a third boy run over by our house."

"That must've been Dave. He always cuts through our garden and jumps the fence to get to his own street. Have they got him yet?"

I shook my head. "The police thought it was you. That's what Chris told them. And they found your pocketknife by Brother MacDonald's window."

"Chris borrowed my knife about a month ago. He said he lost it," Mark explained. "Didn't Chief Reitzen believe you when you told him that I wouldn't do anything like that?"

I was incapable of an honest reply. I said nothing.

"When the trial was over, Chris was really upset, and I guess I was too," Mark continued. "But when you were called to the stake presidency, I began to wonder if maybe the Lord knew something I didn't. But Chris—it drove him crazy. He said the Church was just as corrupt as the law. And for the last few weeks, I've just felt so guilty, knowing what Chris was doing and not doing anything to help those good people. Letting him continue to rob was almost as bad as helping him. But Dad, he's my best friend!"

We sat there quietly in the darkness. The light of the moon was briefly obscured by a dark cloud. The shadow passed, and the light emerged again.

"We'd better go talk to Chief Reitzen. The police are still after you," I said.

He nodded. We stood up and walked together through the darkened streets of our town.

"Dad, I'm sorry for taking all the blackberry leather. I needed something to take with me to eat, and that's the first thing I saw. I know how much you like it. I'll make you a bunch more this summer when they're ripe."

"Sounds good."

"Dad, can I ask you something about work this summer?"

"What?"

"Can you maybe talk to Uncle Ryan and get me my job back?"

"He's still pretty upset. That was a dirty trick you pulled last summer, quitting like that just as he was getting you trained."

"I'm going to need money for my mission. I'd feel guilty if you paid for mine while Matt is paying for his own."

"Why don't I try to get you a job with one of my subs here in the county?"

He shook his head. "Uncle Ryan once said when I was

doing good that if I kept it up, he'd take me into the business if I wanted, help me to be a builder, and eventually turn his business over to me. I know he's ticked at me, but maybe if you talk to him . . ."

"I'll talk to him," I agreed. "We'll see what he says. But what about next fall? Have you decided yet where you're going to go to college? Here at Snow, or the U, or the Y?"

He was quiet for a while. "Dad, would you be ashamed of me if I never went to college?"

I was about to go into my automatic tirade about how he shouldn't squander the gifts he was blessed with, but I kept my peace.

"I know Matt's going to be a lawyer, and Paul's already talking about maybe being a doctor, but would you be ashamed if I was just a builder?"

I fought with myself for a moment. Finally I said, "Your Uncle Ryan's a builder. He's got more bucks than I have, and I've always respected big bucks. But Uncle Ryan also has an engineering degree."

"Don't you think I could make it as a builder without going to school? With you and Uncle Ryan as my teachers?"

"You've got the mind to do a fine job," I agreed at last.

"Then you won't be sore?"

"No," I replied. But it was tough to say.

We walked on until we stopped just outside the police station. A light was still on inside.

"Dad, one more thing."

"What?"

He was silent for a moment as he tried to think of a way to phrase his question. "About the trial, and you helping that guy get off?"

"Yeah?"

"I still don't fully understand."

I put my arm around his shoulder. "Neither do I, son," I admitted.

He opened the door for me and together we went in.